GRATEFUL
LADY

444
CELEBRATORY
EXPRESSIONS OF
GRATITUDE FOR THE
FEMALE BODY:
A SELF-HELP GUIDE
TO A HAPPIER &
HEALTHIER
YOU!

MEHDI ESFANDIARI

MEHDI ESFANDIARI

Contents

Dedication

To the Divine Weaver of Destinies,

In the grand design of existence, every soul that crosses our path is a brushstroke by the Divine Artist. This book is lovingly dedicated to every presence that has graced my journey, especially to Rahila, my cherished companion, whose support has been a manifestation of God's grace in my life.

Each word written, each page turned, and each revelation unveiled could not have been possible without the guiding hand of the Almighty. Rahila, your unwavering belief and love have been the earthly reflection of this divine guidance, a testament to the sacred bond that elevates and inspires. Together with every reader who finds solace and joy in these pages, you embody the tangible hands of God at work in my world.

Your words, your spirit, and your encouragement have been the mirrors of God's compassion and direction. In the monumental and the minute, in the trials and the triumphs, it is through your embodiment of divine love that I have felt the most profound touch of the Creator.

To all who have been beacons on this spiritual odyssey, guiding me toward deeper wisdom and divine intimacy, I offer my profoundest thanks. You are the living expressions of God's grace in my narrative, the human manifestations of His unceasing light.

May this book stand as an ode to the divine role you have all played in the symphony of my life.

With heartfelt appreciation and everlasting gratitude,
Mehdi Esfandiari

Acknowledgements

What is the source of inspiration that propels us forward, fuels our creativity, and lends us the strength to pursue our dreams? For me, unequivocally, the answer is God. In this dedicated space, I pause to express my deep gratitude and reverence for the divine guidance and countless blessings He has bestowed upon me in the creation of this book.

The journey to this moment and the achievements that dot the path are woven from the fabric of God's grace and kindness. He is the mastermind behind my successes, including the nurturing and completion of this book. It was God who sowed the seed of belief in my heart, ensuring I was equipped with the necessary tools, wisdom, and stamina to convert fleeting thoughts into lasting words on these pages.

The divine influence in my life is most vividly seen in the remarkable people I've been fortunate to meet. To those who offered encouragement, lent their support, or held unwavering faith in me - you have been the human embodiment of God's love and motivation. Your impact, whether monumental or subtle, has been critical to my journey, and for this, my gratitude is boundless.

Moreover, my heartfelt thanks extend to you, the reader. Your decision to engage with this book intertwines your story with mine, enriching the narrative of my life. Your interest and the time you devote are gifts I treasure deeply, and it is my sincere hope that these pages offer you joy and revelation, mirroring the fulfillment they've brought me.

Ultimately, this book is a testament to the ceaseless guidance of God and His blessings, made manifest through the kindness and encouragement of those around me. The process of writing this book has been a voyage of personal enlightenment and spiritual affirmation, a voyage that could only be navigated by the light of His grace. Let us all continue to draw from the well of inspiration and strength found in His divine presence.

Introduction

Welcome, dear reader, to a journey that is as much about self-discovery as it is about appreciation. "Grateful Lady" is more than a book; it's a pilgrimage into the heart of gratitude, celebrating the female form in all its complexity, beauty, and strength. This endeavor mirrors the essence captured in "Grateful Man," my companion volume that honors the male form. Together, these books aim to nurture a profound sense of gratitude for the marvels of our physical and spiritual being. Through these pages, we embark on a voyage of acknowledgment and love for the 444 aspects of the female body, each a testament to the divine artistry and wisdom that sculpt us.

Why gratitude, you might wonder? Gratitude transforms how we see ourselves and the world around us. It shifts our focus from what we lack to the abundance we possess, from our challenges to our blessings. This book aims to guide you through a process of recognizing and celebrating the miraculous in the everyday, the divine in the ordinary, the profound in the mundane aspects of our being.

Each chapter of "Grateful Lady" is crafted with care, intending to illuminate a different part of our physical existence, not just from a place of biological function but as a source of spiritual and emotional empowerment. From the strength in our bones, the resilience of our muscles, to the delicate beauty of our skin, every element is explored with reverence and joy. The invitation is to see beyond the physical, to understand our bodies as vessels of life, love, and divine creativity.

The genesis of this book lies in the realization that, in our rush through the demands of daily life, we often forget to pause and appreciate the wonder that is our existence. We overlook the miraculous machinery that works tirelessly to keep us alive, the intricate systems that allow us to experience the world in vivid color, rich sound, and tender touch. "Grateful Lady" seeks to mend this oversight, offering a space to pause, reflect, and give thanks.

Crafted with heartfelt sincerity, this book is a reflection of my own journey in learning to live from a place of gratitude. It is my belief that what we appreciate, appreciates. As such, the pages ahead are filled with expressions of thankfulness for the female body, aiming to inspire a similar sense of appreciation in you. My hope is that, by the end, you will not only find yourself in awe of the divine craftsmanship that is your body but also be moved to cherish and nurture it in new, profound ways.

Moreover, "Grateful Lady" is an ode to the incredible support and guidance I've received along my path, particularly from the divine and the earthly angels in my life, notably my wife, Rahila, who has been a beacon of encouragement and love. It is also a homage to you, the reader, for taking the time to explore these pages and, in doing so, joining me on this journey of gratitude.

As you turn each page, I invite you to keep "Grateful Lady" close, perhaps by your bedside, letting it be the last thing you engage with at night and the first in the morning. In this way, you can end your day with thoughts of gratitude and begin anew with a focus on the abundance you possess. This practice promises to transform not just moments but life itself.

So, let us begin this journey together, with gratitude as our compass and an open heart as our guide. Welcome to "Grateful Lady."

Chapter 1: The Essence of Femininity

Celebrating the Female Form

Welcome to the beginning of a journey that transcends the mere act of living, where each page turned celebrates the intricate beauty and profound depth of the female form. "The Essence of Femininity - Celebrating the Female Form" is not just a chapter; it's an homage to the divine craftsmanship that molds the feminine body, a sanctuary where every curve and contour is revered as a masterpiece of creation.

Within the elegant design of our bodies lies the poetry of existence, a melody composed by the Divine Artisan Himself. Our form, from the gentleness of our curves to the strength within our bones, sings a hymn of gratitude to the Creator, who, with unparalleled wisdom, has intricately woven the essence of femininity into the very fabric of the universe.

This journey is an invitation to embrace the music of our creation, to feel profoundly the grace inherent in our being, and to see ourselves as the embodiment of a divine love story. It is here, in the celebration of womanhood— in all its complexity and simplicity, its resilience and tenderness— that we find a reflection of God's magnificence.

As you delve into the narratives that follow, let your heart be touched by the inherent beauty that is you. This chapter is a tribute to the wonder of womanhood, a canvas where every sentence paints a picture of grace, strength, and divine femininity. May each word serve as a mirror, reflecting the exquisite design crafted by divine hands, resonating with the love of the Creator within your soul, guiding you along the path He has lovingly set forth.

Here, we discover the extraordinary within what may seem ordinary, unveiling beauty in the everyday, and recognizing the divine imprints on every aspect of our existence. This chapter is an affirmation of our essence, an acknowledgment of our value, and a jubilation of our role in the cosmos. It reminds us that we are integral threads in an elaborate, divine tapestry—beautifully created, deeply beloved, and forever held dear by the Creator.

So, let us embark on this path together, with hearts open to love, eyes gazing upon the wonders of creation, and souls tuned to the harmonies of femininity that guide our steps. Let this chapter be an awakening to our divine nature, a rediscovery of the beauty that dwells within and around us.

Welcome, dear reader, to a celebration of femininity, a pause in the sacred space of being, where each breath is cherished, and every heartbeat is a melody in the divine opus of life.

Head

I am deeply grateful for my head, the esteemed crown of my being, located at the very top of my body, serving as the sacred keeper of my thoughts and dreams. It stands as a symbol of my identity, guiding me with wisdom and grace through the tapestry of life, a constant source of pride and joy.

Hair

I hold immense gratitude for my hair, flowing gracefully from my scalp, a vibrant expression of my personal style and femininity. It serves not only as a natural adornment but also as a canvas for creativity and self-expression, bringing me warmth and joy with every strand that dances in the breeze.

Forehead

I am thankful for my forehead, a broad and smooth expanse above my eyes, symbolizing the vastness of my thoughts and the depth of my contemplations. It serves as a bastion of expression, often reflecting my concentration and emotions, inviting understanding and empathy from those around me.

Eyes

My eyes, set like jewels in my face, are wellsprings of gratitude for me. They serve as windows through which I view the wonders of the world, and mirrors reflecting my innermost feelings. Their purpose is not only to see but to communicate silently, revealing my soul's true essence and connecting deeply with those I hold dear.

Ears

I cherish my ears, delicately perched on either side of my head, as they enable me to engage with the world through the harmonies of sound. They are the architects of communication, allowing me to listen, learn, and empathize, enriching my relationships and experiences with the beauty of sound and the subtleties of silence.

Nose

I am filled with gratitude for my nose, the central feature of my face, breathing in the essence of life itself. It is my navigator through the world of scents, from the comforting aroma of home to the natural perfume of a blooming garden, enhancing my experiences and memories with the power of smell.

Mouth

My mouth, the focal point of my face, is a wellspring of gratitude. It allows me to taste the sweetness of life, to voice my thoughts and feelings, and to share smiles and kisses with those I love. Its purpose extends beyond nourishment to become a vessel for love, communication, and expression.

Cheeks

I warmly appreciate my cheeks, which rise and fall with the tides of my emotions, painting my face with the hues of joy, excitement, and affection. They play a crucial role in expressing my innermost feelings without words, making my face a canvas of my heart's silent language.

Chin

For my chin, I hold a special gratitude. Positioned at the base of my face, it provides a balance to my features, symbolizing resilience and determination. It is the touchstone of my facial expressions, playing a subtle yet powerful role in conveying my strength and femininity with grace.

Neck

My neck is a pillar of gratitude, supporting my head with elegance and connecting my thoughts to my heart. It serves as a conduit for voice and breath, carrying my words and laughter to the world, a symbol of strength and flexibility in expressing my truths and emotions.

Shoulders

I am deeply thankful for my shoulders, broad and capable, they carry the weight of my responsibilities with resilience. They embrace the world with strength, offering a shoulder to lean on for comfort and support, a testament to my enduring strength and compassionate nature.

Breasts

My breasts are cherished with gratitude, symbols of femininity and nurture, resting gently on my chest. They represent the nurturing aspect of womanhood, offering comfort and sustenance, and remind me of the deep connections forged through care and love.

Heart

For my heart, I feel profound gratitude. Nestled within my chest, it beats with the rhythm of life, pulsing with love, bravery, and compassion. Its purpose is to sustain me, to feel deeply, and to love boundlessly, a never-ending source of emotional and physical vitality.

Hands

I am forever grateful for my hands, extensions of my being, they create, care, and communicate my intentions and affections. They hold, heal, and express, transforming my thoughts into action and touching the world with kindness and creativity.

Womb

My womb, a sacred space within me, is enveloped in gratitude. It is the cradle of life and creativity, symbolizing the profound power of creation and renewal inherent in womanhood, connecting me to the cycle of life with deep emotional resonance.

Legs

I cherish my legs, the strong foundations that carry me through life's journey. They empower me to move forward with confidence, embodying my independence and strength, allowing me to stand firm and dance freely, celebrating every step of my journey with joy.

Feet

I hold deep gratitude for my feet, for they ground me to the Earth, supporting my every step. They are the foundation of my mobility and freedom, enabling me to walk my path with purpose and grace, connecting me to the grounding energy of the world with every step.

Lips

I am deeply grateful for my lips, the guardians of my expressions and whispers of affection. With their gentle curves, they grant me the power to share beautiful smiles, articulate my thoughts with clarity, and express my most tender emotions. They are the brushstrokes of my femininity, painting my presence with grace and strength.

Eyelashes

My gratitude extends to my eyelashes, the delicate fringes that veil my eyes. They flutter like the soft wings of a butterfly, casting shadows of mystery and allure, enhancing the depth and beauty of my gaze. They protect with elegance, adding a touch of glamour to the windows of my soul.

Eyebrows

I cherish my eyebrows, the natural arches that crown my eyes, framing the artistry of my face. They communicate the unspoken language of my emotions, adding intensity and expression to my gaze. With their refined shape, they underscore my beauty, offering balance and character to my expressions.

Fingernails

For my fingernails, I express gratitude, the petite canvases at my fingertips. They embody my style and attention to detail, offering a glimpse into my personality with their adornment. Strong yet delicate, they are the understated accents of my hands, engaging the world with grace and poise.

Waist

I am thankful for my waist, the soft, defining curve that contours my form. It articulates the harmony of my figure, symbolizing vitality and femininity. This elegant silhouette supports my movements with grace, embodying the fluid dance of life's rhythm, a testament to my strength and flexibility.

Calves

My calves, the sculpted muscles that propel me forward, carry my gratitude. They are the pillars of my steps, whether in a gentle stroll or a spirited run, exemplifying the strength and elegance of my journey. Their form and function celebrate the balance of power and grace, the foundation of my mobility and independence.

Skin

I hold a deep appreciation for my skin, the seamless garment that dresses me in resilience and sensitivity. It is the diary of my life's journey, protective yet open to the world's caress. My skin reflects my inner health and outer beauty, a boundary and a bridge, enveloping me in the unique story of my existence.

Collarbones

I am grateful for my collarbones, the subtle lines that grace the base of my neck, a natural necklace of strength and fragility. They frame my posture with elegance, a delicate edge highlighting the soft power of my femininity, the architectural beauty supporting the canvas of my self-expression.

Eyelids

I am filled with gratitude for my eyelids, the gentle guardians of my eyes. They sweep away weariness and shield my visions, allowing rest and rejuvenation. In their blink lies the simplicity of rest and the power of awakening, a delicate veil that nurtures the windows to my soul with care and protection.

Wrist

For my wrists, I express profound thanks—these slender pillars that bridge my hands to my arms. They enable grace and strength in every gesture, from the writing of love letters to the comforting embrace of a friend. They are symbols of my ability to connect, to create, and to cherish the delicate balance of movement and stability.

Upper Arms

I am sincerely grateful for my upper arms, the strong supports that embrace, lift, and carry through the days. They embody my strength, allowing me to hold my loved ones close and to reach for my dreams. In their embrace, I find the essence of care and the embodiment of resilience, a testament to the loving power I possess.

Lower Legs

My gratitude extends deeply to my lower legs, for they are the sturdy columns that support my every stand and step. With grace, they carry me towards my destinations, grounded in strength yet light with agility. They are the foundation of my movements, from gentle walks to spirited dances, reflecting the journey of my life with steadfast purpose.

Palms

I hold immense appreciation for my palms, the centers of touch and sensation. They are the landscapes of my hands, rich with the ability to feel the world and to give care. Through them, I connect, I comfort, and I create, their lines telling the stories of my life's work and passions. They are the warm embrace, the gentle pat, and the creator's tools, expressions of my heart's intentions.

Soles of the Feet

For the soles of my feet, I feel a deep sense of gratitude. They ground me to the Earth, carrying me on paths known and yet to be discovered. Each step imprinted with the journey of my life, they are the foundation of my physical connection to the world, enabling me to stand firm, to move forward, and to dance freely, celebrating the rhythm of life with every step.

Scalp

I am thankful for my scalp, the fertile ground from which my hair grows, a crown of individuality. It is the unseen protector and nourisher of my hair, responding to my care and touch, and an intimate canvas of sensation. In its health lies the vitality of my hair, reflecting the care I give to myself and the beauty I choose to express.

Neckline

Gratitude fills me for my neckline, the graceful curve that connects my head to my body, framing the strength and delicacy of my form. It is a symbol of poise and elegance, a delicate transition that supports the melodies of my voice and the turns of my head with effortless grace. In its contour, I find the harmonious blend of strength and vulnerability that defines my essence.

Chapter 2: The Graceful Framework

A Tribute to the Skeletal System

E mbark on a voyage into the essence of our strength and grace - the Skeletal System, a sanctuary where every bone is a testament to divine artistry, crafting the framework for our movements and safeguarding the soul of our existence. "The Graceful Framework - A Tribute to the Skeletal System" invites you on an exploration of our structural beauty, where the pillars of our being meld strength with elegance in a ballet of bones.

As you journey through these pages, I invite you to a moment of profound connection with yourself. Trace the storylines etched in your anatomy—the elegance of your collarbones, the protective dome of your skull, the foundational strength of your femurs. Feel the resilience encased within your form, a testament to the beautifully intricate scaffold that supports the dance of life. This tactile engagement is more than an acknowledgment of form; it's a tactile prayer of gratitude for the divine craftsmanship inherent in our design.

Herein, we will uncover the spiritual narratives interwoven with the sinew of our bones—emblems of steadfast strength, dependable support, and dignified resilience that characterize our essence. Every bone, from the subtle grace of our wrists to the empowering arch of our hips, narrates a saga of divine creation, showcasing our innate capacity for healing and regeneration, a reflection of the infinite regenerative grace endowed by the Creator.

This chapter extends beyond mere anatomical appreciation; it is a summons to a deeper realization of our essence. It provides a revered space to ponder and celebrate the skeletal system as an extraordinary divine gift, meticulously crafted, pivotal in our journey toward realizing our physical and spiritual elegance.

Together, let us delve into this homage to form and function, where our appreciation for the skeletal framework evolves into a pathway for profound connections—bridging our faith, our physicality, and our intellect. Through this prism of marvel and thankfulness, we unveil not merely the base of our physical selves but the enduring beauty and deep spirituality that underpin our existence.

Welcome, esteemed reader, to a narrative where each sentence brings us closer to acknowledging the divine grace sculpted into our bones, a narrative of the strength and grace that forge our being. Here, within "The Graceful Framework," we honor the melding of divine purpose with the artistry of the feminine form, a pilgrimage of gratitude resonating with the melody of our creation.

Forehead

I am filled with gratitude for my forehead, the frontal shield of my thoughts and dreams, gracefully arching above my eyes. It is the emblem of contemplation and wonder, beautifully sheltering the wisdom that guides me through life.

Cheekbones

For my cheekbones, I hold deep appreciation, the sculptors of my face's landscape, elevating my smile and carving the contours of joy. These guardians of expression lift not just the structure of my face but elevate my spirits, framing beauty and resilience.

Lower Jaw

I cherish my lower jaw, the bedrock of my verbal expressions and the gatekeeper of nourishment. It grants me the power of speech, the delight of taste, and anchors my smile, a testament to the divine craftsmanship of communication and sustenance.

Skull

My skull, the sacred dome protecting my intellect and spirit, earns my profound gratitude. It cradles the realms of my thoughts and dreams, a divine fortress safeguarding the essence of who I am with elegance and fortitude.

Spinal Bones

I am eternally grateful for my spinal bones, the core pillars of my being, aligning me with strength and poise. They form the backbone of my life's tapestry, supporting me through every movement and moment with steadfast grace.

Neck Vertebrae

For my neck vertebrae, I feel a special kind of thankfulness, enabling the graceful arc of my neck. They support the gentle pivot of my head, nurturing the flow of creativity and inspiration, a bridge between thought and expression.

Upper Back Vertebrae

I treasure my upper back vertebrae, the robust struts supporting my shoulders and chest. This segment of my spine carries the weight of my world with dignity, encasing my heart and lungs in a protective embrace of strength and grace.

Lower Back Vertebrae

My lower back vertebrae receive my heartfelt gratitude, the foundation of my core, offering stability and flexibility. This part of my spine is the bastion of resilience, empowering me to move with confidence and grace through life's myriad paths.

Breastbone

I am thankful for my breastbone, the central protector of my chest, standing guard over my heart and soul. It is a symbol of inner strength and love, a divine guard ensuring the sanctity of life's vital breath and rhythm.

Ribs

For my ribs, I hold deep reverence, the delicate yet strong lattice cradling my heart and breathing life. They form a protective embrace around my vital organs, a testament to the resilience and flexibility that shields and sustains my being's essence.

Pelvic Bones

I embrace my pelvic bones with gratitude, the foundation of my body's structure, cradling the essence of creation. They support my core, offering strength and stability, a testament to the divine design that balances the grace and power of womanhood.

Sacrum

For my sacrum, I hold profound appreciation, the keystone of my spine, anchoring and balancing my body with dignity. It is the sacred bridge that connects my spinal column to the pelvic bones, embodying stability and resilience in every step I take.

Tailbone

I am thankful for my tailbone, the culmination of my spine, a tender reminder of the body's adaptability and evolution. It supports me in sitting and provides a base for the intricate muscles and ligaments that enrich my posture and movement.

Collarbones

I cherish my collarbones, the slender arcs of grace framing the doorway to my heart. They serve as a perch for strength and beauty, a symbol of delicate resilience, supporting the shoulders and linking them to the majesty of my body.

Shoulder Blades

My shoulder blades earn my gratitude, the wings on my back that empower movement and embrace. They float with elegance, enabling the dance of my arms and shoulders, a ballet of strength and flexibility that carries the melody of my actions.

Upper Arm Bones

I am grateful for my upper arm bones, the pillars of my arms' strength, lifting, holding, and embracing the world. They are the support for my movements, enabling the grace and power of my gestures, from the tender to the bold.

Radii

I am thankful for the radii in my forearms, the elegant pillars on the thumb side that allow me to reach out and grasp the world with grace. They enable the dexterity of my hands, allowing me to write my story, touch my loved ones, and carry my dreams with strength.

Ulnae

For my ulnae, the steadfast supports on the little finger side of my forearms, I hold deep appreciation. They partner seamlessly with the radii, providing the strength to embrace life's challenges and the delicate power to hold onto what matters most.

Carpals

My gratitude extends to my carpals, the intricate assembly of wrist bones that dance in harmony, enabling the fluid movements of my hands. They are the gatekeepers of flexibility and motion, allowing me to express myself through gestures, work, and the tender touch of care.

Femora

I am grateful for my femora, the pillars of strength in my thighs, bearing the essence of my movement and stability. They support me as I stand, walk, and dance through life, a testament to endurance and the joy of motion.

Fibulae

For my fibulae, the slender companions to my tibiae, I am thankful. They add to the symphony of my legs' strength and grace, supporting my movements with subtlety and providing a balance that enables my strides and stands.

Tarsals

My tarsals, the cornerstone of my ankles, receive my gratitude for their role in my balance and agility. They are the pivotal points that connect my world-walking feet to the foundation of my legs, a beautiful example of functional harmony.

Metatarsals

I am profoundly grateful for my metatarsals, the framework of my feet that bear the weight of my dreams and journeys. They ground me to the earth, enable my steps towards the future, and dance in the rhythm of my life's song, supporting me with every move I make.

Phalanges

I cherish my phalanges within my toes, the delicate architects of balance and grace in my feet. Each bone a testament to the intricate dance of steps and stability, allowing me to tiptoe through life's beauty and stand firmly in my truths.

Calcanei

For my calcanei, the foundational stones of my heels, I am deeply grateful. They anchor my stance, empowering each step with strength and resilience, a robust base for the journeys I undertake and the paths I choose to explore.

Nasal Bones

I am thankful for my nasal bones, the protectors of my breath's gateway, shaping the character of my face. These small but significant bones form the bridge of my nose, a symbol of resilience and elegance in the face of life's breezes and storms.

Lacrimal Bones

My lacrimal bones, nestled in the corners of my eyes, receive my heartfelt gratitude. Guardians of my tears, they house the wells of my emotions, allowing for the expression of joy, sorrow, and the beauty of vulnerability.

Palatine Bones

I appreciate my palatine bones, the silent keystones at the back of the roof of my mouth. They form the chamber of taste and speech, a hidden sanctuary for the words I speak and the flavors that narrate the stories of my life.

Inferior Nasal Conchae

For my inferior nasal conchae, the intricate scroll-like bones within my nose, I hold deep gratitude. They temper the breath of life, filtering and humidifying air, a subtle yet profound blessing in every inhalation.

Vomer

I am grateful for the vomer, the slender plow that divides the inside of my nose. It shapes the currents of my breath, a central part of the symphony of senses that guides me through the fragrances and whispers of the world.

Ethmoid Bone

My ethmoid bone, cradled at the roof of my nose, earns my admiration for its delicate structure and vital role. It is a labyrinth of air and sense, a sacred space for the resonance of breath and the subtleties of smell.

Sphenoid Bone

I cherish my sphenoid bone, the keystone at the base of my skull, a hidden supporter of my brain's foundation. Its intricate form is a marvel of creation, cradling my thoughts and dreams at the crossroads of soul and body.

Temporal Bones

For my temporal bones, the sides and base of my skull, I am profoundly thankful. They are the temples of my hearing and balance, encasing the delicate symphony of sound and the grace of equilibrium that tunes me to the rhythms of the universe.

Occipital Bone

My occipital bone, at the back and base of my skull, receives my gratitude for its role as the backdrop of my mind. It safeguards the pathways of my vision, a sturdy cradle for the precious globe of thought and dreams.

Parietal Bones

I hold reverence for my parietal bones, the broad canvases on the sides and roof of my skull. They form the dome of my being, a protective vault for the treasures of my intellect and the vast landscapes of my imagination.

Maxilla

I am grateful for my maxilla, the stronghold of my upper jaw. It is the foundation of my smile, the altar of my speech, and the cradle of my taste, a harmonious blend of function and beauty, supporting the expressions that connect me to the world.

Hyoid Bone

I am grateful for my hyoid bone, nestled gracefully in my neck, the anchor of speech and swallow. This unique bone supports the harmony of my voice and the nourishment of my body, a symbol of communication and strength held gently in the curves of my being.

Os Coxae

For my os coxae, the elegant hip bones that include the ilium, ischium, and pubis, I hold immense appreciation. They are the cradle of my posture, the bearers of my body's weight as I sit, stand, and move through life, embodying the essence of support and feminine grace.

Metacarpals

I cherish my metacarpals, the pillars within my hands that enable me to grasp the world in all its texture and form. They empower me to touch, to create, and to express love through action, a testament to the delicate strength in my grasp.

Femur

My gratitude extends deeply to my femur, the robust pillar of my thigh, a foundation of movement and stability. It supports my steps, my runs, and my leaps, a testament to the enduring strength and dynamic grace that propels me forward.

Patella

I appreciate my patella, the small but mighty protector of my knee joint. It glides with my movements, ensuring flexibility and strength in each bend and stretch, a guardian of my mobility and a symbol of resilience in my journey.

Tibia

For my tibia, the steadfast shin bone, I am deeply thankful. It bears the essence of my stride, a beacon of support guiding me through paths untrodden and roads well-worn, a testament to the enduring journey of life.

Fibula

I am grateful for my fibula, the slender ally to my tibia, cradling the muscles of my calf. It whispers of balance and agility, supporting me quietly yet effectively as I navigate the dance of life with poise and determination.

Cervical Vertebrae

My cervical vertebrae, the delicate vertebrae in my neck, earn my heartfelt gratitude. They bear the weight of my thoughts and dreams, allowing the gentle nod of agreement, the turn of curiosity, and the tilt of contemplation, connectors of mind and body.

Thoracic Vertebrae

I hold deep appreciation for my thoracic vertebrae, the sturdy pillars of my upper back. They cradle my heart and lungs, forming a protective embrace around the organs that breathe life and love, a backbone of strength and care.

Lumbar Vertebrae

For my lumbar vertebrae, the powerful segments of my lower back, I am profoundly thankful. They support the core of my being, enabling me to bend and lift, to stand tall in my convictions, and to flex with the winds of change, embodying resilience and grace.

Chapter 3: The Symphony of Movement

Honoring the Muscular System

I n the grand orchestra of our being, "The Symphony of Movement - Honoring the Muscular System" plays a captivating melody that speaks to the essence of motion and grace inherent in the female form. Within this chapter, we delve into the exquisite network of muscles that orchestrate every gesture, every step, and every embrace with which we engage the world. From the subtle flexing of our fingers to the powerful strides of our legs, each movement is a note played in the divine concert of existence, a testament to the miraculous engineering bestowed upon us.

As you traverse the narratives and insights laid out in these pages, I invite you to embark on a tactile journey of self-discovery. Engage with the living tapestry of your muscles, exploring the resilience, the tenderness, and the strength that pulse beneath your skin. This act of exploration is more than a physical encounter—it is a sacred communion with the temple of your body, transforming each moment of awareness into a personal testament to the miracle of your design.

Beyond the marvel of physical capability, we celebrate the muscles for their symbolic resonance—symbols of the enduring capacity to face life's challenges with grace, to carry our burdens with fortitude, and to offer solace with gentle touch. Our expressions of gratitude become a chorus of admiration for the delicate balance our muscles maintain, a harmony of might and softness that enables us to experience life's rich tapestry in its fullness.

This chapter extends an invitation to view the muscular system not merely as a mechanism of movement but as a profound expression of our connection to the divine. It is here, in the interplay of strength and vulnerability, that we find a reflection of our spiritual journey, a narrative of resilience, grace, and divine intention woven into the very fibers of our being.

Let "The Symphony of Movement" be a transformative exploration that deepens your appreciation for the incredible capabilities of your body. May it illuminate the path to recognizing your strength—both seen and unseen—as a divine gift to be nurtured and celebrated. Herein lies an opportunity to honor the physical expressions of our spirits, to embrace the joy, the power, and the grace that animate our every move.

Welcome, dear reader, to an immersive experience that not only reveals the intricacies of the muscular system but also honors the beauty and spiritual depth of our existence. Through this exploration, may you discover the resonant beauty of your own movement, each step a note in the endless melody of creation, every breath a rhythm in the eternal dance of life.

Orbicularis Oculi - Eyes

I am filled with gratitude for my Orbicularis Oculi, the delicate muscles framing my eyes, allowing me to express the depth of my emotions through every glance and blink. These muscles, encircling the windows to my soul, enable me to see the world's beauty and convey warmth and compassion without uttering a single word.

Zygomaticus Major and Minor

I cherish my Zygomaticus Major and Minor, the architects of my smile, painting expressions of joy and happiness on my face. These muscles are the essence of my laughter and the silent bearers of my inner joy, lifting my spirits and those around me with the simple, universal gesture of a smile.

Masseter

My gratitude extends to my Masseter muscles, guardians of my jawline, bestowing strength and definition. They empower me to speak, to taste life's flavors, and to express myself fully, framing the resilience and grace that define my visage.

Temporalis

I am thankful for my Temporalis muscles, contributing to the contour of my jawline, a symbol of determination and eloquence. These muscles, working in harmony, enable me to communicate my thoughts and feelings, reinforcing my ability to connect and engage with the world.

Orbicularis Oris

With deep appreciation, I honor my Orbicularis Oris, the muscles that define my lips, the vessel of my voice, and the bearer of my kisses. They allow me to speak words of love, to smile, and to express a myriad of emotions, painting my feelings onto the world.

Buccinator

I am grateful for my Buccinator muscles, nestled within my cheeks, the unseen sculptors of my face's silhouette. They assist in my expressions and my enjoyment of food, playing a subtle yet significant role in the moments that fill my life with flavor and joy.

Frontalis

My Frontalis, the canvas of my forehead, receives my gratitude for its role in expressing my wonder, concern, and curiosity. This muscle allows me to convey empathy and understanding, creating a bond of shared experiences with those I encounter.

Platysma

I express my gratitude for my Platysma, draping gracefully over my neck and jawline, enhancing my profile with elegance. This muscle reflects the strength and flexibility in my voice and stance, a testament to the power of gentleness.

Sternocleidomastoid

I cherish my Sternocleidomastoid muscles, defining the contours of my neck, symbols of resilience and grace. They support my head, allowing me to turn and face the world with confidence, embodying the balance between strength and beauty.

Trapezius

Gratitude flows to my Trapezius, the broad canvas across my shoulders and upper back, pillars of my posture. This muscle is the cloak of my strength, supporting me as I carry the world's weight with dignity and helping me stand tall amidst life's challenges.

Deltoid

I am deeply grateful for my Deltoid muscles, sculptors of my shoulders and upper arms, lending a graceful curve that symbolizes strength and femininity. These muscles empower me to lift, reach out, and embrace the vastness of life with open arms.

Pectoralis Major

With heartfelt gratitude, I acknowledge my Pectoralis Major, foundational to the elegance of my chest and bust line, offering support and poise. They remind me of the heart's proximity, the center of love and courage that I carry within.

Biceps Brachii

I cherish my Biceps Brachii, symbols of strength and the ability to pull my dreams closer to reality. These muscles, shaping my upper arms, enable me to embrace my loved ones tightly, blending strength with tenderness.

Triceps Brachii

My gratitude extends to my Triceps Brachii, the essence of my upper arm's silhouette, allowing me to push forward through challenges. They represent my capacity to give back, to extend support, and to reach out into the world with confidence.

Brachialis

I am thankful for my Brachialis, hidden yet powerful, contributing to the refined definition of my arms. This muscle underlines the importance of inner strength, supporting my actions and gestures with grace and purpose.

Latissimus Dorsi

Gratitude fills my heart for my Latissimus Dorsi, the wide wings of my back that contribute to the allure of a tapered waist, embodying the grace and strength of my spirit. They enable me to draw my dreams closer, embracing life's opportunities with vigor.

Rectus Abdominis

I am grateful for my Rectus Abdominis, the core of my physical and inner strength, sculpting a toned belly that stands as a testament to my dedication and discipline. This muscle is my powerhouse, fueling my actions with energy and determination.

External and Internal Obliques

With appreciation, I honor my External and Internal Obliques, artists carving the definition of my waist, symbols of flexibility and adaptability. They twist and turn with life's rhythms, guiding me through change with resilience.

Transversus Abdominis

My deepest thanks to my Transversus Abdominis, the deepest layer of my core, fortifying my center with strength and stability. This muscle wraps around me like a gentle embrace, grounding me in my power and poise.

Erector Spinae

I express profound gratitude for my Erector Spinae, the pillars of my back, upholding my posture with dignity and strength. They remind me to stand tall, to face the horizon with hope, and to carry the weight of my aspirations with grace.

Gluteus Maximus

I am immensely thankful for my Gluteus Maximus, the foundation of my form, providing shape and support. This muscle carries me forward, a steady and strong base from which I move through life, embracing each step with confidence and vitality.

Gluteus Medius and Minimus

I treasure my Gluteus Medius and Minimus for sculpting the contours of my buttocks, offering stability and grace with every step. They are the unsung heroes that support my body's balance, enabling me to move with confidence and elegance.

Quadriceps Group

With joy, I celebrate my Quadriceps, the powerhouse at the front of my thighs, shaping the tone and vitality of my legs. These muscles empower me to leap forward, to sprint towards my dreams, embodying the strength of my strides.

Hamstrings Group

I am filled with gratitude for my Hamstrings, crafting the shapely silhouette of the back of my thighs. They are the rhythm in my steps, the push and pull that propel me forward, blending flexibility with force.

Adductor Group

My appreciation extends to my Adductor Group, defining the inner contours of my thighs, enhancing my leg's harmony and symmetry. They are the quiet keepers of my stability, guiding my path with precision and grace.

Sartorius

I am grateful for my Sartorius, the longest muscle, draping elegantly across my thigh, a subtle architect of my leg's aesthetics. This slender muscle weaves strength and beauty, enabling the dance of life with each movement.

Gastrocnemius

Deep thanks to my Gastrocnemius, the bold curve of my calves, symbolizing the leap of faith and the groundedness in my journey. These muscles are the expression of my will, driving me forward, upwards, into the realm of possibilities.

Soleus

I cherish my Soleus, nestled beneath the Gastrocnemius, for sculpting the fullness of my calves, a testament to enduring strength and resilience. It whispers the tales of journeys taken, of landscapes explored with steadfast dedication.

Tibialis Anterior

My Tibialis Anterior, guarding the front of my shin, receives my gratitude for its role in defining the contours of my lower leg. This muscle underscores my steps with precision, a guardian of my balance, enabling me to walk with purpose and poise.

Peroneal Muscles

I am thankful for my Peroneal Muscles, shaping the side of my lower leg, their strength and flexibility enriching my movement. They are the subtle sculptors of form, enabling agility and adaptation, supporting my ventures with courage.

Flexor and Extensor Muscles of the Foot

Gratitude blossoms for my Flexor and Extensor Muscles of the foot, the caretakers of my arches, facilitating grace in my steps. They are the harmonizers of my movement, the bridge between my body and the earth, embodying balance and support.

Intrinsic Foot Muscles

My Intrinsic Foot Muscles, nestled within my feet, are treasured for their role in strength and balance, the unsung heroes of every step I take. They ground me, remind me of my journey's foundation, enabling me to stand firm and poised.

Pelvic Floor Muscles

With heartfelt gratitude, I honor my Pelvic Floor Muscles, the foundation of my core's strength and stability. They are the silent pillars of my inner temple, supporting me from within, enhancing my vitality and inner harmony.

Diaphragm

I am profoundly thankful for my Diaphragm, the rhythm of my breath and the stabilizer of my core. This muscle is the essence of life's breath, a reminder of the power of pause, of inhalation and exhalation, sustaining my essence with grace.

Levator Scapulae

Gratitude fills me for my Levator Scapulae, from neck to shoulder, shaping the elegance of my posture and neck contour. They are the carriers of grace, enabling me to lift my head high, to face the world with dignity and assurance.

Rhomboid Muscles

I cherish my Rhomboid Muscles, architects of my upper back's contour and posture. These muscles weave strength and structure, a tapestry of resilience that supports the canvas of my back, enabling me to carry the beauty of confidence.

Intercostal Muscles

With joy, I acknowledge my Intercostal Muscles, nestled between my ribs, crafting the definition of my ribcage. They play the vital tune of breath, a symphony of life that resonates within, reminding me of the fluidity and grace in each breath taken.

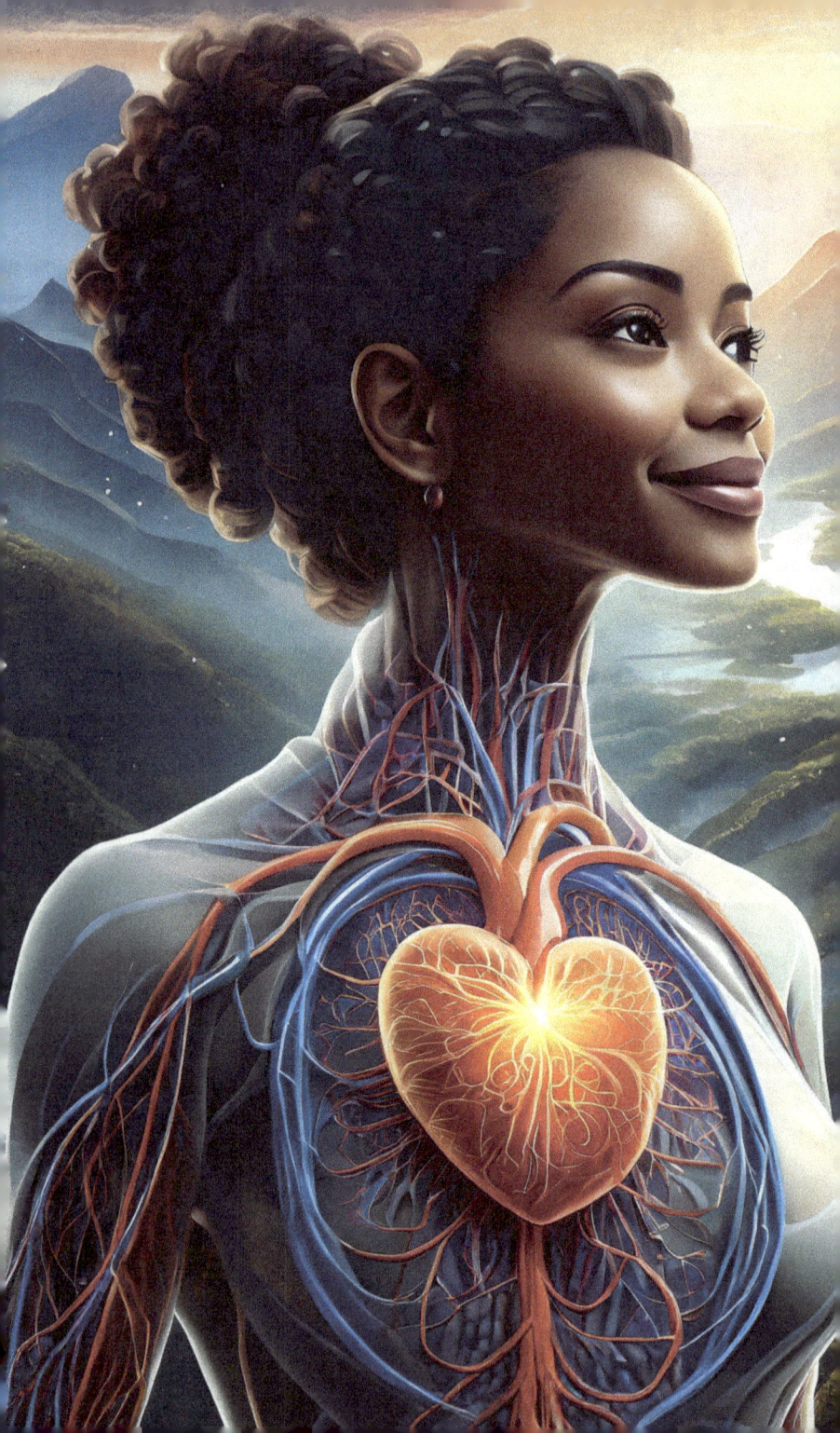

Chapter 4: The Rhythms of Life

Exploring the Circulatory System

D ive into the river of life that flows within us - our Circulatory System, an exquisite network designed by the divine to nourish, sustain, and rejuvenate every cell of our being. As we journey through this chapter, we marvel at the heart's rhythmic beat, a drumming echo of God's miraculous engineering, propelling life through rivers and streams of blood, a testament to His infinite love and wisdom.

In this exploration, let the pulse beneath your fingertips remind you of the continuous blessings coursing through your veins. Each heartbeat, a whisper of life, invites a reflection on the sacred flow of health and vitality that gratitude amplifies. Recognizing the wonders of our circulatory paths is an intimate dance with the divine, a celebration of the life force that binds us to the universe and each other.

Embracing gratitude for our heart and vessels transforms our perspective, ushering in healing waves that cleanse, mend, and fortify our spirits and bodies. This practice of thankfulness is a beacon of empowerment, illuminating the strength and resilience woven into our fabric. The daily ritual of acknowledging this divine gift encourages a journey towards holistic well-being, enriching our lives with peace, health, and a profound connection to the sacred rhythm of existence.

Beyond the physical marvel that is our circulatory system, lies a metaphor for the interconnectedness of life itself. Just as our blood vessels form an intricate web of pathways, so too are our lives intertwined with those around us, sharing in the universal circulation of energy, love, and compassion. This realization opens our hearts to the profound impact of our existence, not just within our bodies but in the world at large. We are reminded that every act of kindness, every gesture of love, is a ripple in the vast ocean of life, nourishing the collective soul of humanity.

This chapter also invites us to ponder the silent language of the heart, an organ that speaks not in words but in beats, a rhythm that resonates with the core of our being. As we delve deeper into the workings of our circulatory system, we discover lessons in resilience, adaptability, and unconditional support—qualities that our hearts exemplify with every throb. It is a call to live heartfully, embracing the pulsating rhythm of life with courage, compassion, and an open heart, ready to receive and spread the blessings that flow from the fountain of gratitude.

Let this chapter inspire you to weave gratitude into the essence of your daily life, recognizing the Circulatory System not just as an anatomical marvel but as a spiritual bridge to deeper health, harmony, and divine communion. Herein lies the power to transform routine into ritual, infusing your days with the magic of appreciation and the promise of renewal. As we navigate the pathways of our circulatory system, may we also navigate the pathways of life with grace, gratitude, and a deep-seated reverence for the divine orchestration that keeps us bound in a beautiful symphony of existence.

Heart

I'm filled with gratitude for my heart, the beacon of love and vitality within me. Every beat sings a melody of life, sustaining me with every pulse. It's a symbol of unyielding strength and compassion, enabling me to live fully and love deeply.

Aorta

My deepest thanks go to my aorta, the main artery that spreads life's essence through me. It ensures vitality reaches every part of my body, empowering me to thrive and flourish in every moment of my journey.

Coronary Arteries

I appreciate my coronary arteries, guardians of my heart's well-being. They supply the lifeblood that keeps my heart beating with fervor, reminding me of the beauty of care and connection.

Pulmonary Arteries

Gratitude for my pulmonary arteries, the pathways that carry hope to be renewed in my lungs. They symbolize the beautiful exchange between taking in and letting go, teaching me balance and renewal.

Pulmonary Veins

Thankful for my pulmonary veins, returning revitalized life to my heart. They represent renewal and the fresh breath of opportunities, encouraging me to welcome each new experience with a rejuvenated spirit.

Superior Vena Cava

Grateful for the superior vena cava, channeling wisdom from above back to my heart. It reminds me of the importance of gathering life's lessons and bringing them home, enriching my soul and spirit.

Inferior Vena Cava

I cherish my inferior vena cava, bringing experiences from my body's lower parts back to the heart. It teaches me to integrate and reflect upon life's journey, grounding me in wisdom and humility.

Jugular Veins

My gratitude extends to the jugular veins, for returning the essence of thought and vision to the heart. They remind me of the connection between mind, body, and soul, enriching my life with depth and understanding.

Carotid Arteries

I am grateful for my carotid arteries, nourishing my brain and senses. They enable me to think, dream, and perceive the beauty around me, celebrating the gift of awareness and cognition.

Subclavian Arteries

Appreciation for my subclavian arteries, supplying life to my arms. They empower me to embrace life, offer help, and create beauty, celebrating the strength and capability within me.

Subclavian Veins

Thankful for my subclavian veins, carrying the experiences of touch and action back to my heart. They teach me the beauty of giving and receiving, highlighting the cycle of love and contribution.

Brachial Arteries

Gratitude for my brachial arteries, fueling my arms with the energy to act and embrace. They remind me of my capacity to reach out, to build, and to cherish, weaving the tapestry of my interactions.

Radial Arteries

I am thankful for my radial arteries, guiding vitality to my hands. They enable me to touch, heal, and connect, celebrating the power of human contact and the magic in the simplest gestures.

Ulnar Arteries

Grateful for my ulnar arteries, supplying life to the paths less traveled in my arms. They teach me the value of support in all endeavors, ensuring strength and flexibility in every action.

Palmar Arches

My thanks to the palmar arches, cradling the power of creation in my hands. They represent the ability to mold my reality, to care, and to express love through the work of my hands, honoring the artistry in daily life.

Femoral Arteries

I cherish my femoral arteries, vital pathways that support my ability to stand tall and move forward. They fuel my steps with strength and grace, reminding me of the journey I walk and the independence I hold dear.

Popliteal Arteries

Gratitude for my popliteal arteries, nestled behind my knees, they are the unseen force that bends and flexes with life's demands. They teach me resilience and the beauty of moving with ease and adaptability.

Tibial Arteries

Thankful for my tibial arteries, bringing vitality down to my lower legs. They ground me, support my stride, and remind me of my connection to the earth, empowering each step with purpose and stability.

Dorsalis Pedis Arteries

Appreciation for my dorsalis pedis arteries, the pulse of life at the top of my feet. They remind me of the delicate balance in moving forward and the intricate dance of steps that compose my journey.

Great Saphenous Veins

Grateful for my great saphenous veins, the long vessels that traverse the length of my legs. They symbolize the long journeys, the deep connections to my path, and the endurance within my spirit.

Small Saphenous Veins

Thankful for my small saphenous veins, guiding the flow from the outer paths back to my heart. They teach me the value of perspective, the beauty in the details, and the strength in subtlety.

Renal Arteries

My deepest thanks to my renal arteries, the providers of life to my kidneys. They remind me of the power of purification and renewal, essential for balance and well-being in my life's journey.

Renal Veins

I am grateful for my renal veins, returning the gift of cleansing from my kidneys. They represent the cycle of renewal, the release of what no longer serves, and the embrace of nourishment and clarity.

Hepatic Arteries

Appreciation for my hepatic arteries, nourishing my liver, the source of vitality and detoxification. They remind me of the importance of nurturing and caring for myself, ensuring resilience and vitality.

Hepatic Veins

Gratitude for my hepatic veins, channels of relief and purification from my liver. They teach me the beauty of letting go, of refining and releasing, to emerge cleaner, clearer, and more vibrant.

Hepatic Portal Vein

Thankful for my hepatic portal vein, the connector of nourishment and cleansing. It stands as a testament to transformation, to the alchemy of turning what I consume into energy and light.

Mesenteric Arteries

I cherish my mesenteric arteries, providers to my intestines, where nutrients become part of me. They symbolize growth, nourishment, and the conversion of sustenance into the energy that fuels my passions and dreams.

Splenic Artery

Gratitude for my splenic artery, supplying life to my spleen, the guardian of my vitality. It reminds me of the strength in filtering, in distinguishing what will nourish from what must be refined.

Splenic Vein

Thankful for my splenic vein, carrying away the remnants of a day's work. It teaches me the value of cleansing, of making space for the new, and the continuous cycle of renewal and regeneration.

Gastric Arteries

I express my gratitude for my gastric arteries, the life-givers to my stomach, enabling the first steps of nourishment and transformation. They remind me of the importance of nurturing myself with care, turning sustenance into the energy that sparks my vitality.

Gastric Veins

Thankful for my gastric veins, channels of cleansing from the stomach, they play a crucial role in the journey of renewal, teaching me the beauty of transformation and the strength found in processing and renewal.

Capillaries

My capillaries, the delicate network where life's smallest exchanges happen, receive my deepest appreciation. They symbolize the intricate connections between all aspects of my being, facilitating the dance of life at its most fundamental level.

Lymphatic Vessels

Gratitude fills me for my lymphatic vessels, the silent pathways of cleansing and immunity. They represent the body's resilience, quietly protecting and purifying me, a reminder of the strength in gentle, consistent care.

Semilunar Valves

I cherish my semilunar valves, guardians of my heart's rhythm and flow. They ensure that every beat moves life forward, teaching me the power of progress and the importance of letting life unfold with grace and precision.

Atrioventricular Valves

Thankful for my atrioventricular valves, the custodians of my heart's chambers, they exemplify coordination and timing, ensuring that every moment and every heartbeat is an opportunity for synchronicity and harmony.

Intercostal Arteries

Appreciation for my intercostal arteries, nurturing the spaces between my ribs, they remind me of the support structure that breathes life into every action, every word, and every embrace.

Lumbar Arteries

Gratitude for my lumbar arteries, which support my lower back, the foundation of my strength and flexibility. They remind me of the importance of a strong foundation, empowering me to stand tall and move with confidence.

Iliac Arteries

My iliac arteries, gateways to the lower limbs, receive my gratitude for supplying the essence of movement and stability. They encourage exploration and adventure, reminding me of the journey's joy and the steps I take in search of growth and discovery.

Iliac Veins

Thankful for my iliac veins, returning life's experiences from the lower limbs, they symbolize the journey's cycle, the return home enriched by every step, every leap, and every stride.

Cephalic Vein

I am grateful for my cephalic vein, a prominent pathway on the outer arm, representing the strength to reach out to the world and the courage to grasp new opportunities with openness and enthusiasm.

Basilic Vein

Appreciation for my basilic vein, running along my arm's inner side, it stands as a symbol of inner strength and the flow of creativity and love from the depths of my heart to the tips of my fingers.

Median Cubital Vein

Gratitude for my median cubital vein, the connector at the crook of my elbow, a reminder of the intersections in life, where paths cross, and new directions are chosen, symbolizing flexibility and adaptability.

Deep Veins of the Limbs

Thankful for the deep veins of my limbs, hidden yet vital carriers of my journey's essence. They teach me the beauty in depth, in the unseen paths that support and nourish, ensuring strength and stability from within.

Arterioles

I cherish my arterioles, the small arteries that lead to life's exchange sites. They remind me of the importance of attention to detail, the small steps that lead to significant changes, and the gentle guidance needed to navigate life's complexities.

Venules

I express gratitude for my venules, the gentle collectors of life's essence from the capillary exchange, guiding it back to the heart. They teach me the value of gathering experiences, processing them with care, and preparing for the next cycle of life.

Endothelium

Thankful for my endothelium, the inner lining of my blood vessels, a seamless barrier that delicately manages the flow of life within me. It reminds me of the power of boundaries, protecting and nurturing my inner world with grace and intelligence.

Vascular Smooth Muscle

Gratitude fills me for my vascular smooth muscle, the strength within my blood vessels, allowing them to respond and adapt to life's demands. They embody resilience, the ability to stand firm yet flex with life's pressures and challenges.

Pericardium

I cherish my pericardium, the protective sac encasing my heart, a symbol of safeguarding what is most precious. It teaches me the importance of self-care and the strength found in vulnerability, protecting the heart of my being.

Myocardium

Appreciation for my myocardium, the powerful muscle of my heart, beating the rhythm of life. It reminds me of my inherent strength and capacity for love, propelling me through life with courage and passion.

Endocardium

Grateful for my endocardium, the inner lining of my heart, where blood touches the heart's essence. It symbolizes the intimate connections in life, the moments of contact that enrich and transform my journey.

Sinoatrial Node

I am thankful for my sinoatrial node, the natural pacemaker of my heart, setting the pace for life's dance. It teaches me the importance of rhythm, the balance between action and rest, guiding me through life's fluctuations with grace.

Atrioventricular Node

Gratitude for my atrioventricular node, the electrical relay that keeps my heart's rhythm in sync. It represents harmony and coordination, reminding me that every part of my life works best when connected and in tune.

Bundle of His and Purkinje Fibers

I appreciate the Bundle of His and Purkinje fibers, pathways of electrical impulses that ensure my heart beats as one. They symbolize unity and connection, the intricate network that binds my being in harmony and purpose.

Chordae Tendineae

Thankful for my chordae tendineae, the heartstrings that hold my valves in place, teaching me the strength of connections, the ties that ground me, ensuring I can open and close my heart with resilience and grace.

Papillary Muscles

Gratitude to my papillary muscles, anchoring the heart's chords, ensuring the valves function smoothly. They remind me of the importance of support systems, the strength found in the foundations that keep me grounded and secure.

Thoracic Aorta

Appreciation for my thoracic aorta, the main highway of life through my chest, fueling my journey with vitality. It teaches me about life's pathways, the importance of nourishing every part of myself with what enriches and sustains.

Abdominal Aorta

I am grateful for my abdominal aorta, supplying life's essence to my lower regions. It symbolizes the core of my being, the center from which life flows, reminding me to nurture my foundation with care and attention.

Celiac Plexus

Thankful for my celiac plexus, the network of nerves near my heart, a reminder of the complex interplay between heart and mind. It teaches me the power of intuition, the subtle signals that guide my decisions and path.

Circle of Willis

Gratitude for the Circle of Willis, a circulatory loop that ensures my brain is nourished, symbolizing resilience and adaptability. It reminds me of the interconnectedness of life, the strength found in support and flexibility.

Lenticulostriate Arteries

Appreciation for my lenticulostriate arteries, small vessels that penetrate deep into my brain, reminding me of the intricate beauty of life's design. They teach me to cherish the hidden depths within, the unseen strengths that support my journey.

Chapter 5: The Breath of Vitality

Appreciating the Respiratory System

S tep into the sanctuary of breath in "Breath of Life," where we celebrate the divine gift of air that fills our lungs, the sacred wind that sustains our essence. This chapter invites you to immerse in the miracle of respiration, a delicate ballet orchestrated by God, allowing us to draw in life's energy and sing out our existence.

As you journey through these pages, let each inhalation be a prayer of thanks, and every exhalation, a release of what no longer serves you. This conscious engagement with our breath is a profound act of gratitude, acknowledging the unseen force that animates us, a gentle reminder of the Creator's presence in every moment.

The act of cherishing our breath revitalizes our spirit, nurturing a garden of peace within. It's a potent form of healing, soothing our minds, enriching our souls, and purifying our bodies. By embracing gratitude for our Respiratory System, we unlock a wellspring of vitality, cultivating resilience and serenity in our lives.

This chapter is more than an exploration; it's an invitation to transform breathing into a ritual of gratitude, enriching your daily practice with mindfulness and divine awareness. The benefits of this practice extend beyond the physical, opening doors to spiritual growth, emotional balance, and a harmonious life, deeply connected to the rhythm of creation.

In deepening our understanding and appreciation for this vital system, we also recognize the intricate beauty of the body's design—a testament to the meticulous care in our creation. The Respiratory System, a marvel of efficiency and grace, mirrors the balance and harmony inherent in the natural world. It reminds us of our connection to all living things, bound together by the breath of life, each inhale a shared sustenance, and each exhale a contribution back to the world.

Furthermore, this awareness prompts a reverence for the environment that sustains us, urging a stewardship rooted in gratitude. Protecting the quality of the air we breathe becomes not just an act of self-care but a sacred duty, a tangible expression of our gratitude for life's breath bestowed upon us by the divine.

Let the Breath of Life guide you to a deeper appreciation of your divine human experience, empowering you to infuse every day with the healing power of gratitude. Herein, discover the key to a life lived fully, breath by breath, a beautiful habit that nourishes the soul and brings you closer to God's eternal grace. Through this chapter, may you find a renewed sense of awe for the simple yet profound act of breathing, embracing it as a daily reminder of life's fragility, beauty, and the omnipresent love of the Creator.

Nasal Cavity

I'm filled with joy for my nasal cavity, a sanctuary nestled within my face, warming and purifying the air that fuels my life. Its purpose, to safeguard my breath, fills me with a sense of protection and love, reminding me of the care imbued in every part of me.

Nostrils

I cherish my nostrils, the charming gatekeepers at the very forefront of my being, welcoming the breath of life into me. They give me the power to experience the world's fragrances, connecting me to memories and moments, and making me feel deeply anchored in the present and beautifully alive.

Pharynx

Gratitude warms my heart for my pharynx, a vital passage in my throat, guiding nourishment and air on their essential journey. It stands as a testament to the seamless integration of life's basics, making me feel whole, nourished, and vibrantly connected to my existence.

Larynx

I am grateful for my larynx, cradled in my throat, the birthplace of my voice. It allows me to express my thoughts, my love, and my song, enriching my connections with others and empowering me to stand strong in my truth, feeling both heard and profoundly loved.

Trachea

My trachea, the steadfast tube descending beneath my throat, earns my heartfelt thanks. It conducts the air that sustains me, a constant and reliable presence that supports my every breath, making me feel strong, capable, and gracefully alive.

Bronchi

I embrace my bronchi, the airways branching within my chest, distributing life's vital air to each lung. Their purpose, to ensure every breath reaches deep within, fills me with gratitude for the intricate beauty of my body, feeling beautifully complex and wonderfully designed.

Bronchioles

For my bronchioles, the delicate pathways threading through my lungs, I hold immense gratitude. They carry the whispers of breath to the alveoli, making me feel intricately connected to the fabric of life, each breath a tapestry of joy and vitality.

Alveoli

My alveoli, the tiny air sacs nestled in my lungs, are treasures that exchange life's oxygen for every exhale's gift. They remind me of the magic in the simple act of breathing, making me feel deeply connected to the cycle of life, cherished, and part of something greater.

Lungs

I express deep gratitude for my lungs, the delicate yet powerful organs resting in my chest. With every breath, they embrace life's air, sustaining me with oxygen and vitality. This miraculous process fills me with a profound sense of wonder and gratitude, making me feel vibrant and energetically alive.

Pleura

My heartfelt thanks go to the pleura, the protective layers wrapping my lungs in a tender embrace. Their seamless movement allows me to breathe effortlessly, a silent testament to the body's grace and resilience, making me feel secure, nurtured, and lovingly held.

Diaphragm

I cherish my diaphragm, the mighty muscle that dances beneath my lungs, orchestrating the rhythm of my breath. Its movements, gentle yet powerful, fill me with life, reminding me of the strength and grace that lies within, making me feel empowered and joyfully alive.

Intercostal Muscles

Gratitude fills me for my intercostal muscles, woven between my ribs, aiding in the subtle expansion of my chest. With each breath, they remind me of life's interconnectedness, making me feel deeply woven into the tapestry of existence, supported and beautifully resilient.

Rib Cage

I hold immense gratitude for my rib cage, the sturdy haven safeguarding my heart and lungs. Its protective embrace fills me with a sense of security and strength, reminding me of my inner fortitude and the beauty of being sheltered and cherished.

Nasal Conchae

For the nasal conchae, nestled within my nose, I am thankful. These delicate structures warm and filter the air I breathe, connecting me to the world in the most intimate way. They make me feel cared for and connected, a beautiful reminder of the body's wisdom and grace.

Epiglottis

I am grateful for my epiglottis, the vigilant guardian at the gateway of my breath and nourishment. It ensures each journey is safe, making me feel protected and loved, a subtle yet profound reminder of the body's intricate care and thoughtful design.

Thyroid Cartilage

My thanks go to the thyroid cartilage, the structure that graces the front of my neck. It not only supports my voice but also serves as a shield, making me feel both expressive and protected, embodying the strength and resilience that characterize my essence.

Carina

I express gratitude for the carina, the critical fork in my trachea that guides air into each lung. It stands as a symbol of life's diverging paths, reminding me of the beauty in each breath and decision, making me feel guided, purposeful, and lovingly directed.

Mediastinum

For the mediastinum, the central haven within my chest, I am deeply thankful. Home to my heart and other vital structures, it reminds me of the central role love and life-force play in my existence, making me feel centered, cherished, and vibrantly alive.

Sinuses

I appreciate my sinuses, the air-filled spaces that resonate with my voice and lighten the weight of my head. They connect me to the subtleties of sensation and sound, making me feel uniquely attuned to life's harmonies, beautifully resonant and alive.

Cricoid Cartilage

Gratitude fills me for the cricoid cartilage, the ring-like structure supporting my airway and voice. It stands as a symbol of strength and flexibility, making me feel secure in my expression and breath, embraced in the melody of life.

Arytenoid Cartilages

I am thankful for the arytenoid cartilages, small yet significant, they play a crucial role in my voice's modulation. They enable the richness and diversity of my expressions, making me feel wonderfully complex and capable of creating beautiful symphonies of sound.

Vocal Folds

My vocal folds, the delicate bands that allow me to speak, sing, and shout, fill me with gratitude. They are the instruments of my soul's expression, enabling me to connect deeply with others and the world around me, making me feel profoundly understood and lovingly heard.

Tracheal Rings

I am grateful for the tracheal rings, the sturdy protectors of my airway. Their resilience ensures my breath's passage is safe and unobstructed, allowing me to embrace life's essence. This strength fills me with confidence, knowing I am supported in every moment.

Pulmonary Capillaries

My deepest thanks to the pulmonary capillaries, the delicate threads of life that weave oxygen into my blood. In their embrace, every breath turns into energy, a magical transformation that sustains my being, making me feel marvelously alive and interconnected.

Respiratory Mucosa

I cherish the respiratory mucosa, the guardian lining of my airways. It filters and humidifies each breath, protecting me with every inhalation. This silent sentinel makes me feel cared for and nurtured, enveloped in a blanket of gentle protection.

Nasopharynx

For the nasopharynx, the pathway that connects my nose to my throat, I express gratitude. It is the gatekeeper of breath and sound, playing a key role in my health and communication. This connection makes me feel integrated and whole, a beautiful blend of function and harmony.

Oropharynx

I am thankful for the oropharynx, the passageway that escorts air and food, blending the essentials of life. It stands at the crossroads of nourishment and breath, reminding me of life's simple pleasures and the joy found in every breath and bite.

Laryngopharynx

Gratitude fills me for the laryngopharynx, the conduit to the esophagus and larynx. It guides nourishment and air, ensuring my survival and voice. This pathway makes me feel deeply connected to the essence of life and the power of expression.

Glottis

I appreciate the glottis, the vibrant gateway to my vocal cords. It is the birthplace of my voice, allowing me to express thoughts, emotions, and dreams. This ability to communicate fills me with joy and gratitude, making me feel heard and connected.

Paranasal Sinuses

My thanks to the paranasal sinuses, the resonant chambers that enrich my voice and lighten my head. Their function, subtle yet impactful, enhances my senses and well-being, making me feel uniquely attuned and vibrantly alive.

Lung Lobes

I express deep appreciation for my lung lobes, the segments that expand with life's breath. Each lobe plays a vital role in filling me with vitality, a constant reminder of the body's capacity to renew and thrive, making me feel vibrant and full of life.

Hilum of Lung

Gratitude for the hilum of the lung, the gateway through which breath enters and exits. It stands as a testament to the complexity and beauty of life, ensuring that I am nourished by the air around me, making me feel deeply connected to the world's rhythm.

Surfactant

I am profoundly thankful for surfactant, the miracle substance that keeps my airways open with each breath. Its presence is a reminder of the body's intricate design and care, making me feel marvelously supported and effortlessly buoyant.

Accessory Muscles of Respiration

My heartfelt thanks to the accessory muscles of respiration, the helpers that assist in my breath's ebb and flow. Their strength and flexibility empower me, especially in moments of effort, making me feel resilient, capable, and wonderfully alive.

Chapter 6: The Tapestry of Sensation

Delving into the Nervous System

E mbark on a journey into the essence of connection and perception in "Symphony of Senses," a heartfelt ode to the Nervous System, the divine orchestra conducted by God's hand. This chapter unfolds the mystery and magic of how we sense, understand, and interact with the world around us, a testament to the intricate design and boundless love of our Creator.

As we delve into the wonders of the Nervous System, let yourself be amazed by the seamless communication within your body, a harmonious symphony that enables thought, emotion, movement, and sensation. Each nerve, each synapse, plays its note perfectly, creating the melody of your experience, a melody composed by God's genius.

In recognizing the marvels of our neural pathways, we touch the divine spark within us, fostering a profound gratitude for the unseen threads that connect us to life's tapestry. This gratitude illuminates the mind's power, the heart's wisdom, and the soul's depth, encouraging a healing journey that transcends the physical.

This exploration is an invitation to witness the sacred dance of stimuli and responses, a celebration of the body's ability to feel, react, and adapt. It's a call to honor the Nervous System as more than just a network of cells and signals; it's the divine infrastructure of our very essence, enabling us to perceive God's creation in its full glory.

Let this chapter be a transformative experience that deepens your relationship with your inner self and the world around you. Through the lens of gratitude, discover the resilience, beauty, and power embedded in your Nervous System. Embrace this practice as a daily ritual, a path to holistic well-being, spiritual awakening, and a richer, more vibrant life connected to God's infinite grace.

Brain

I'm filled with immense gratitude for my brain, the master orchestrator of my thoughts, emotions, and movements. Its incredible complexity enables me to dream, to reason, and to love, making me feel deeply connected to the wonders of life and the essence of my being.

Spinal Cord

Thankful for my spinal cord, the vital pathway of communication between my brain and body. It ensures that every sensation and movement is gracefully coordinated, making me feel whole, empowered, and beautifully in sync with the rhythm of life.

Cerebrum

I cherish my cerebrum, the seat of intelligence, creativity, and decision-making. Its intricate folds and vast networks gift me with the power to imagine, to learn, and to evolve, filling me with a profound sense of wonder and endless possibilities.

Cerebellum

Gratitude fills me for my cerebellum, the guardian of balance and grace in my movements. It fine-tunes my actions, allowing me to move through the world with ease and confidence, making me feel harmoniously balanced and elegantly poised.

Brainstem

I am grateful for my brainstem, the foundation of life's most essential functions. It breathes life into every moment, regulating my heartbeat and breath, reminding me of the preciousness of existence and the beauty of living each day with intention.

Thalamus

Appreciation for my thalamus, the great relay station of my brain. It filters and directs sensory information, enabling me to experience the world in all its richness, making me feel deeply attuned to my surroundings and vibrantly alive.

Hypothalamus

Thankful for my hypothalamus, the conductor of my body's orchestra, maintaining harmony and balance. It regulates my hunger, thirst, and emotions, connecting me to my inner world with wisdom and care, making me feel nurtured and understood.

Limbic System

I hold deep gratitude for my limbic system, the emotional heart of my brain. It weaves the fabric of my feelings and memories, enriching my life with depth and color, making me feel passionately alive and profoundly connected to the ones I love.

Frontal Lobe

I express my gratitude for my frontal lobe, the captain of my consciousness. It empowers me with the ability to plan, to speak, and to dream, making me feel in control of my destiny and boldly creative in the tapestry of my life.

Parietal Lobe

Thankful for my parietal lobe, the center of perception and awareness. It allows me to navigate the world, to feel and understand, blending the physical with the mental in a dance of sensation and cognition, making me feel deeply in tune with the universe.

Occipital Lobe

Gratitude for my occipital lobe, the realm of vision and sight. It translates light into images, allowing me to see the beauty of the world, making me feel blessed with the gift of vision, to witness life's artistry and to cherish the visual memories that color my existence.

Temporal Lobe

I am deeply thankful for my temporal lobe, the keeper of sounds and the harvester of words. It holds my memories and enables me to understand language, weaving the symphony of voices into the fabric of my experience, enriching my connections and interactions.

Motor Cortex

Gratitude floods me for my motor cortex, the sculptor of movement and action. It commands my muscles with precision, enabling me to express myself through movement, dance, and touch, making me feel dynamically alive and masterfully expressive.

Sensory Cortex

I cherish my sensory cortex, the canvas of sensation. It paints my world with touch, temperature, and pain, allowing me to experience the tactile richness of life, making me feel intimately connected to the world around me.

Prefrontal Cortex

I'm grateful for my prefrontal cortex, the architect of my personality and the predictor of my future. It shapes my decisions, my social interactions, and my moral judgments, endowing me with the ability to envision my future and connect deeply with others.

Basal Ganglia

Appreciation envelops me for my basal ganglia, the conductor of my habits and movements. It streamlines my actions, making them more efficient and effortless, allowing me to perform with grace and agility, making me feel skilled and adept.

Hippocampus

Thankful for my hippocampus, the guardian of my memories. It navigates my past, informing my present and shaping my future, making me feel rooted in my experiences and enriched by my life's journey.

Amygdala

I hold gratitude for my amygdala, the wellspring of my emotions. It colors my world with the hues of joy, fear, love, and sorrow, making me feel vibrantly alive and deeply connected to the essence of human experience.

Neurons

Gratitude for my neurons, the messengers of my being. They transmit the electrical impulses that dictate my thoughts, actions, and feelings, making me marvel at the miracle of my existence and the intricate web of connectivity that defines me.

Synapses

I am thankful for every synapse, the spaces where communication blossoms. They are the junctions of thought and action, the birthplaces of learning and memory, making me feel endlessly capable of growth and connection.

Neurotransmitters

Appreciation for my neurotransmitters, the chemical couriers of my brain. They modulate my mood, my thoughts, and my bodily functions, making me feel balanced and alive, dancing to the rhythm of life's complex biochemistry.

Peripheral Nerves

Thankful for my peripheral nerves, the emissaries to my body. They extend the central commands to every corner, making me feel connected and responsive, a unified being in action and sensation.

Somatic Nervous System

I express gratitude for my somatic nervous system, the mediator of voluntary movement. It empowers me to interact with the world, to embrace, to act, making me feel in control and capable of affecting my world.

Autonomic Nervous System

Gratitude for my autonomic nervous system, the silent regulator of my body's states. It keeps my heart beating, my breath flowing, without conscious thought, making me feel marvel at the unconscious wisdom that sustains me.

Sympathetic Nervous System

I am deeply grateful for my sympathetic nervous system, the mobilizer of my body's rapid responses. It primes me for action, energizes me in moments of need, and makes me feel powerfully alive, ready to meet the world with vigor and resilience.

Parasympathetic Nervous System

With heartfelt thanks, I appreciate my parasympathetic nervous system, the restorer of peace and balance. It soothes and calms me after the storm, guiding me back to a state of tranquility and stability, making me feel nurtured and cared for by my own body.

Cranial Nerves

Gratitude embraces my cranial nerves, the conduits of my senses and movements. They connect me to my surroundings, enabling me to taste, see, hear, and express, making me feel deeply engaged with the vibrant tapestry of life.

Spinal Nerves

I cherish my spinal nerves, the pathways of sensation and action. They bridge my body and brain, allowing me to interact with the world with dexterity and sensitivity, making me feel beautifully synchronized and adept.

Ganglia

Thankful for the ganglia, the hubs of neural activity outside my central nervous system. They process and modulate my responses, making me feel connected and responsive to the subtle nuances of my environment.

Sensory Receptors

Deep appreciation for my sensory receptors, the scouts of sensation. They alert me to touch, pain, temperature, and all the nuances of the external world, making me feel richly attuned to the diverse textures of life.

Meninges

Gratitude for my meninges, the protective layers of my central nervous system. They safeguard my brain and spinal cord, making me feel secure in the knowledge that a vital shield stands guard over my most precious assets.

Cerebrospinal Fluid

I am thankful for the cerebrospinal fluid, the cushion of my brain and spinal cord. It protects and nourishes my central nervous system, making me feel supported and preserved in a fluid embrace.

Blood-Brain Barrier

Appreciation for my blood-brain barrier, the vigilant gatekeeper of my brain. It carefully selects what may enter, ensuring my neural environment is kept safe and stable, making me feel protected from harm and secure in my internal haven.

Vagus Nerve

Gratitude blossoms for my vagus nerve, the wanderer that connects my heart, lungs, and gut to my brain. It mediates my body's relaxation responses, making me feel deeply connected within myself, a harmony of body and mind.

Dermatomes

Thankful for the dermatomes, the map of sensory territories on my skin. They enable me to pinpoint sensations, making me feel intricately woven into a tapestry of touch, each thread uniquely felt and acknowledged.

Myelin Sheath

I treasure my myelin sheath, the insulator of my neurons. It speeds up the transmission of electrical impulses, making me feel efficient and swift in thought and reaction, a marvel of biological engineering.

Glial Cells

Deep gratitude for my glial cells, the unsung heroes of my nervous system. They support, nourish, and protect my neurons, making me feel nurtured from the inside out, a testament to the complexity and care within my being.

Reflex Arc

Thankful for the reflex arc, the pathway of instinctive responses. It protects me with immediate reactions, making me feel secure in the knowledge that my body has its own innate wisdom, ready to act in my defense.

Broca's Area

I am grateful for Broca's Area, nestled within the frontal lobe, a cradle of my ability to express thoughts through language. Its remarkable orchestration allows me to communicate my dreams, love, and aspirations, connecting me deeply with those around me.

Wernicke's Area

Thankful for Wernicke's Area, located in the temporal lobe, which gifts me the power of understanding. Through it, I embrace the words of the world, finding meaning and connection in the cascade of sounds that reach my ears, enriching my relationships and learning.

Pineal Gland

With gratitude, I acknowledge my Pineal Gland, a beacon in the brain's darkness, regulating the rhythms of sleep and wakefulness. Its silent work in the night guides my journey into dreams, ensuring rest and renewal for the body and soul.

Olfactory Bulbs

I cherish my Olfactory Bulbs, gateways to memories and emotions, through which the fragrance of life flows. They bring me the scents of nature, loved ones, and cherished moments, weaving a tapestry of sensory memories that color my world.

Optic Nerves

I am immensely grateful for my Optic Nerves, the channels of light and vision, connecting the eyes to the brain's depths. Through them,

I witness the world's beauty, the faces of loved ones, and the words that guide my path, painting my days with the hues of life.

Auditory Nerves

With deep appreciation, I thank my Auditory Nerves, which carry the symphony of sounds from the world into the essence of my being. They allow me to hear laughter, music, and the subtle whispers of nature, enriching my life with auditory tapestries.

Gustatory Cortex

I express gratitude for my Gustatory Cortex, which unveils the spectrum of flavors, from the sweetness of love to the bitterness of sorrow. It enables me to savor the diversity of foods, celebrating the rituals of dining and the joys of culinary exploration.

Somatosensory Association Cortex

I am thankful for my Somatosensory Association Cortex, a realm where touch, warmth, and texture are woven into the fabric of my consciousness. It binds me to the physical world, allowing me to feel the embrace of a loved one and the caress of the wind.

Motor Association Cortex

With gratitude, I honor my Motor Association Cortex, the planner of my every motion. It is the architect of my actions, from the steps that carry me forward to the embrace that signals love, empowering me to interact with the world with intention and grace.

Mirror Neurons

I am grateful for my Mirror Neurons, the silent empaths within, that resonate with the actions and emotions of others. They are the underpinning of my capacity to empathize, to feel connected to the joy and pain of others, nurturing the bonds that unite us as beings.

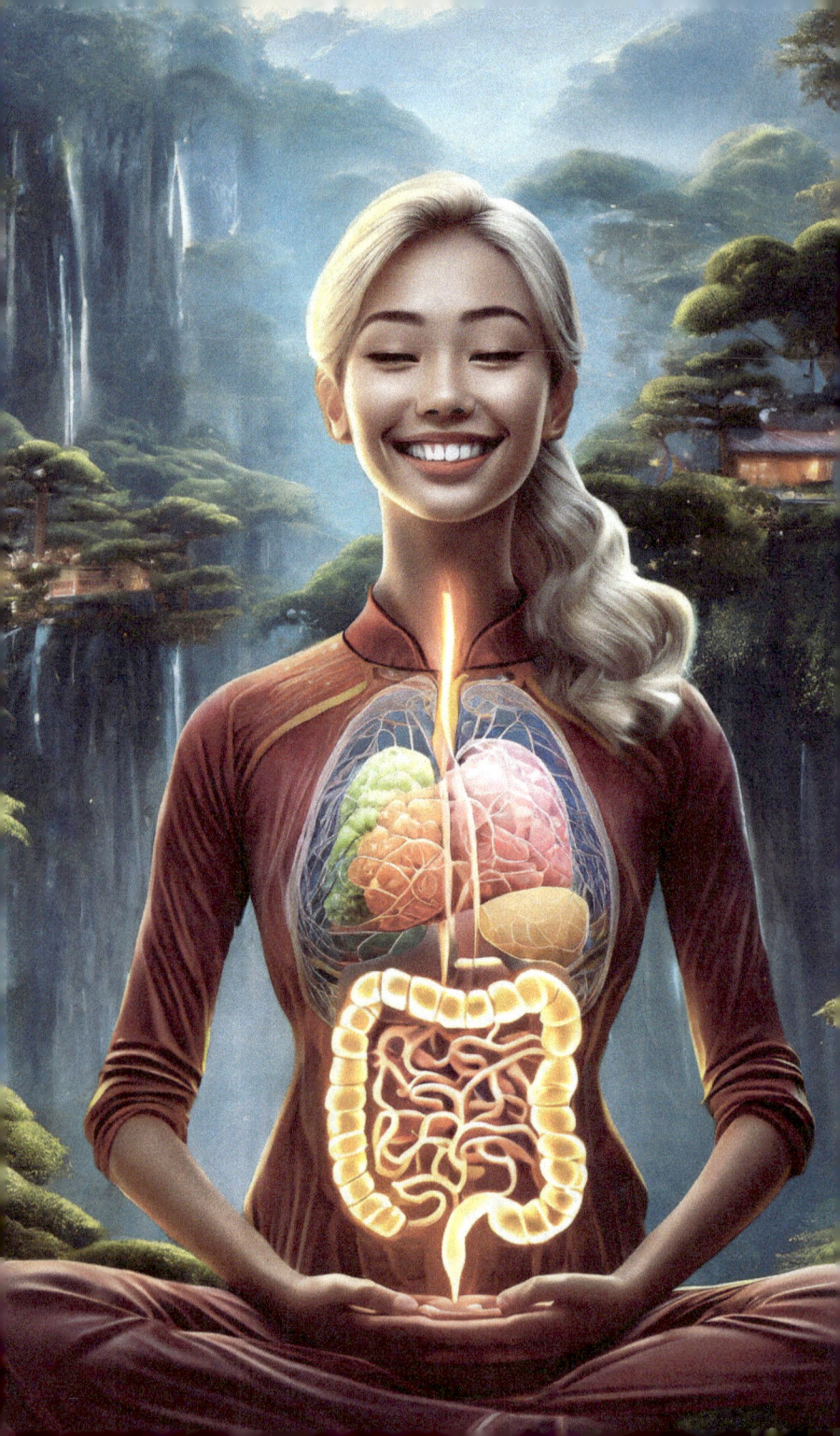

Chapter 7: The Journey of Nourishment

Valuing the Digestive System

Welcome to "Nourishment for the Soul," an exploration of the Digestive System as a metaphor for the divine cycle of receiving, transforming, and giving back. This chapter invites you on a heartfelt journey through the wondrous process that turns food into energy, sustenance into life, guided by God's intricate design and loving intent.

Each bite we take is a testament to life's interconnectedness, a sacred exchange between us and the earth, blessed by the heavens. As we delve into the complexities of our digestive tract, from the first touch of food on our lips to its transformation into vital energy, let us be filled with gratitude for this miraculous process that sustains our physical being and fuels our journey through life.

In recognizing the marvels of our Digestive System, we uncover layers of spiritual symbolism—the power of gratitude to transform, the importance of absorbing what nourishes us, and the grace in letting go of what does not. This system, designed by God, teaches us about balance, renewal, and the sanctity of the body as a temple that houses our soul.

Let this chapter be a reminder of the divine presence in the everyday act of eating, an act that connects us to the broader web of creation, to the farmers who till the land, to the hands that prepare our meals, and to the Divine who provides for all. It's an invitation to see our meals as a form of prayer, a moment to pause, give thanks, and reflect on the abundance we are given.

Embrace the journey through "Nourishment for the Soul" as an opportunity to cultivate a deeper appreciation for your body's capabilities and for the food that nourishes you. Allow this gratitude to be a source of healing and strength, empowering you to make choices that honor your body and spirit. Through mindful eating and thankful living, we connect more deeply with ourselves, with each other, and with God, finding true nourishment for the soul.

Mouth

I am grateful for my mouth, the vibrant gateway to nourishment and expression, located at the very center of my face. It allows me to savor the flavors of life, to communicate my thoughts and laughter, and to bestow kisses of love, making me feel joyful, expressive, and deeply connected.

Salivary Glands

For my salivary glands, I hold appreciation, for they facilitate the first step in digestion and keep my mouth comfortably moist. Their role in preparing the food that sustains me and enabling the clarity of my speech fills me with gratitude, making me feel nurtured and articulate.

Pharynx

I cherish my pharynx, a vital passageway in my throat for both nourishment and breath. It stands at the crossroads of essential functions, making me feel alive with every swallow and every word spoken, celebrating the simplicity of being.

Esophagus

Deep thanks to my esophagus, the steadfast conduit that guides nourishment from my mouth to my stomach. It serves with silent diligence, allowing me to enjoy the pleasure of eating with ease, making me feel gracefully cared for and content.

Stomach

My stomach is a source of heartfelt gratitude, the strong yet gentle organ that turns nourishment into energy. It works with quiet might,

fueling my every action and emotion, making me feel powerful, energized, and lovingly sustained.

Small Intestine

I am thankful for my small intestine, the winding path where nutrients
are embraced and absorbed. It is the unseen hero in my abdomen,
gifting me the vitality from my meals, making me feel wonderfully
nourished and vibrant.

Large Intestine

For my large intestine, I feel profound appreciation. It completes
the journey of digestion, reclaiming water and preparing for renewal,
making me feel balanced, whole, and in harmony with my body's
natural rhythms.

Rectum

Gratitude fills me for my rectum, the reservoir at the end of digestion.
It functions with quiet respect, playing a crucial role in balance and
health, making me feel secure in its reliability and the body's intelligent
design.

Anus

I am grateful for my anus, a part of my body that completes the
vital process of digestion. It does so with discretion and efficiency,
contributing to my overall well-being, making me feel confident and
comfortable in my body's natural processes.

Liver

My liver, the master chemist of my body, earns my endless gratitude. It purifies and produces, balancing and nourishing, a true guardian of my vitality, making me feel cleansed, strong, and wonderfully intricate in its divine complexity.

Gallbladder

I hold appreciation for my gallbladder, the small organ that aids in digestion with the precision of timing and release. It supports me quietly, ensuring the breakdown of my meals is smooth and efficient, making me feel supported and harmonized with every healthy choice.

Pancreas

I am grateful for my pancreas, tucked away in the curve of my belly, a dual-purpose marvel of my digestive and endocrine systems. It is a font of enzymes and hormones, essential for turning food into fuel and keeping my blood sugar in check, a bastion of balance that makes me feel energized and harmoniously regulated.

Appendix

My appendix, a small pouch off the cecum, I now know plays its part in my immunity. For its role as a haven for beneficial bacteria, I am appreciative, understanding that it contributes to my body's defenses, making me feel resilient and cared for in the most extraordinary ways.

Gastroesophageal Sphincter

I cherish my gastroesophageal sphincter, the vigilant gatekeeper between my esophagus and stomach. Its rhythmic opening and closing allow me to enjoy meals without discomfort, a subtle yet essential role that fills me with comfort and gratitude.

Pyloric Sphincter

Gratitude flows for my pyloric sphincter, the portal at the exit of my stomach, meticulously timing the passage of digested food. It ensures that my digestion proceeds with grace, making me feel at ease, trusting in the precision of my body's intricate processes.

Ileocecal Valve

I am thankful for my ileocecal valve, the faithful sentinel that stands between my small and large intestines. It diligently regulates the flow, maintaining harmony within, making me feel assured and fluent in the dance of digestion.

Mucosa

For the mucosa lining my digestive tract, I feel deep appreciation. This tender layer absorbs nutrients and protects my tissues, a testament to the body's thoughtful design, which fills me with wonder and gratitude for its silent, nurturing work.

Villi

My villi, the tiny projections in my small intestine, deserve my heartfelt thanks. They vastly expand the landscape where nutrients join my body, making me feel profoundly nourished and grateful for this microcosm of absorptive ingenuity.

Microvilli

I hold admiration for my microvilli, the minute extensions of my villi that further maximize nutrient absorption. They represent the intricate details of my wellbeing, making me feel amazed and cherished down to the smallest aspect of my being.

Cecum

I appreciate my cecum, the commencement of my large intestine, a chamber where digestion takes a new course. It marks the transition from absorption to elimination with care, making me feel grateful for its role in the final stages of my nourishment.

Ascending Colon

For my ascending colon, I am grateful. It bears the task of further extracting water and salts from the remnants of meals, a vital phase in digestion that makes me feel supported and sustained in the cycle of health.

Transverse Colon

Gratitude envelops my transverse colon, the bridge across my abdomen where digestion's journey continues. It plays a crucial part in processing life's sustenance, making me feel connected across my body's landscape, assured in its steadfast function.

Descending Colon

I am thankful for my descending colon, the diligent pathway that guides digestion's progress downward. It quietly compacts what remains, preparing for the final stages of recycling and renewal, which fills me with a sense of completeness and gratitude for my body's efficiency.

Sigmoid Colon

My gratitude blossoms for my sigmoid colon, the S-shaped curve that is the penultimate phase of digestion. It acts with a gentle rhythm, ensuring that waste is processed with care, which makes me feel respected and attuned to the natural rhythms within me.

Mesentery

I appreciate my mesentery, the intricate web that anchors my intestines, providing them with support and nourishment through its blood vessels. This unsung hero of my abdomen is vital for my well-being, and I'm grateful for its silent, steadfast provision.

Omentum

For my omentum, the apron-like tissue draped over my abdominal organs, I feel a warm thankfulness. It plays a protective and fat-storing role, a guardian of my internal balance, which makes me feel secure in the knowledge of its protective presence.

Oral Cavity

I cherish my oral cavity, the entrance hall to digestion and a chamber of communication. It allows me to taste the richness of life and articulate my words with clarity, making me feel joyful for the symphony of flavors and conversations it permits.

Tongue

I hold deep gratitude for my tongue, a muscle teeming with taste buds and the agility for speech. It lets me savor life's variety and express my thoughts and feelings, making me feel vibrant and connected through the gifts of taste and language.

Teeth

My teeth earn my heartfelt thanks for their strength in breaking down food and their role in shaping my smile. They stand as the stalwarts of my oral cavity, making me feel confident and thankful for every nourishing bite and every radiant smile.

Gums

I am grateful for my gums, the soft framework that cradles my teeth. They provide a firm foundation and play a crucial role in my oral health, making me feel nurtured and appreciative of their resilient support.

Hard Palate

For my hard palate, I express appreciation. It forms the firm section of the roof of my mouth, aiding in the mechanics of eating and speaking, which makes me feel grounded in the essentials of nourishment and communication.

Soft Palate

I cherish my soft palate, the flexible back part of the roof of my mouth. It's instrumental in swallowing and speaking, making me feel in awe of the delicate coordination that allows me to enjoy the seamless blending of functions.

Uvula

Gratitude swells for my uvula, the small yet significant pendulum that plays a part in speech and swallowing. It reminds me of the body's attention to detail, making me feel fascinated and thankful for the small things that make a big difference

Oropharynx

I am thankful for my oropharynx, the middle section of my throat, where the paths for air and food cross. Its role in guiding sustenance and breath fills me with joy and gratitude for the intricacies of my body's design.

Laryngopharynx

My laryngopharynx, where digestion and respiration pathways diverge, earns my appreciation. It's a crucial juncture for my wellbeing, harmoniously managing life's essentials, making me feel secure and gracefully coordinated.

Bile Ducts

I am thankful for my bile ducts, the vital channels for the flow of bile necessary for digestion. They work in silent harmony with my liver and gallbladder, making me feel grateful for their role in my body's symphony of sustenance.

Hepatic Portal Vein

For my hepatic portal vein, which diligently transports nutrient-rich blood from my digestive organs to my liver, I feel immense gratitude. It is an essential part of my nourishment process, making me feel wonderfully connected and nurtured.

Sphincter of Oddi

I hold deep appreciation for my Sphincter of Oddi, a muscular valve controlling the flow of digestive juices. Its precise regulation allows for efficient digestion, making me feel grateful for this small yet significant contributor to my digestive harmony.

Brunner's Glands

Gratitude fills me for my Brunner's glands, which quietly secrete protective mucus in my small intestine. They provide a shield for my digestive tract, making me feel cared for in a very intimate way.

Peyer's Patches

I cherish my Peyer's patches, the specialized lymphoid tissue in my small intestine that protects me from pathogens. They are guardians of my immune system, making me feel loved and safeguarded from within.

Crypts of Lieberkühn

I am grateful for my Crypts of Lieberkühn, the intestinal glands playing a role in secretion and absorption. They are an example of the unseen yet crucial workings of my body, making me feel intricate and wonderfully complex.

Anal Sphincters

My anal sphincters earn my respect and thanks for their control and regulation, a testament to my body's wisdom in maintaining balance and health. They give me confidence and peace of mind, allowing me to feel secure and dignified in my body's natural processes.

Chapter 8: The Harmony of Balance
Understanding the Endocrine System

E mbark on an enlightening passage through "Harmonizing Essence," a chapter dedicated to the elegance and subtlety of the Endocrine System. This narrative celebrates the divine intricacy of our hormonal harmony, a melody composed by God, performed by our bodies, resonating with the rhythms of life itself.

The Endocrine System, with its silent whispers, orchestrates a dance of molecules that touch every corner of our being, influencing our growth, mood, metabolism, and reproduction. It's a testament to the unseen forces that shape our existence, mirroring the unseen hand of the Creator who delicately balances all aspects of the universe.

As we explore the glands and hormones that constitute this system, let's imbue our hearts with gratitude for the silent guidance and gentle nudges that keep us aligned with our highest selves. Each hormone, a messenger of love and balance, speaks to the cells in a language crafted by divine wisdom, ensuring that life flows within us with grace and purpose.

In recognizing the silent work of our Endocrine System, we are reminded of God's omnipresence in the smallest details, orchestrating our lives' vast symphony with precision and care. This system teaches us about the power of subtlety, the strength in gentleness, and the profound impact of what lies beneath the surface.

Let "Harmonizing Essence" inspire you to listen more deeply to your body and spirit, to seek balance in your life, and to appreciate the exquisite composition of your being. It's an invitation to trust in the divine process, to find peace in the knowledge that we are beautifully designed and lovingly maintained by forces both within us and beyond us.

This chapter is more than an exploration of biological functions; it's a journey towards understanding how gratitude for our internal harmony can illuminate our path to well-being, guide us towards inner peace, and connect us more profoundly with the divine grace that sustains us all.

Hypothalamus

I am deeply grateful for my hypothalamus, nestled within my brain, the master regulator of my body's internal balance. It orchestrates the symphony of hormones, ensuring my heart rate, sleep cycles, appetite, and emotions harmonize beautifully. Its unseen guidance enriches my daily life, allowing me to experience the world with vitality and emotion.

Pituitary Gland

To my pituitary gland, the tiny yet mighty beacon of hormonal control perched at the base of my brain: thank you. You tirelessly oversee growth, reproduction, and metabolism, crafting the essence of my femininity and strength. Your delicate work empowers me, molding my body's resilience and grace.

Pineal Gland

With heartfelt appreciation, I honor my pineal gland, the secluded pine-cone-shaped gem in my brain. You paint my nights with dreams by releasing melatonin, guiding me into peaceful slumber. In your quietude, you connect me to the rhythmic cycles of nature, blessing me with rest and rejuvenation.

Thyroid Gland

I am profoundly thankful for my thyroid gland, the vigilant guardian of my metabolism, nestled in the front of my neck. Your whispers of hormones fuel my every cell with energy, kindling the fires of vitality and warmth within me. In your balance, I find strength and a zest for life, radiating health and well-being.

Parathyroid Glands

To my parathyroid glands, the discreet sentinels behind my thyroid, guardians of my bones' strength and my blood's balance: your quiet diligence in regulating calcium levels gifts me with a strong frame and a steady heart. I cherish the unseen stability you provide, a foundation for life's dance.

Adrenal Glands

I celebrate my adrenal glands, perched atop my kidneys like crowns, the source of my resilience and drive. In moments of challenge, you flood me with adrenaline, igniting my courage and determination. Your cortisol rhythms sustain me through life's ebbs and flows, imbuing me with enduring strength.

Adrenal Cortex

Gratitude fills me for my adrenal cortex, the outer layer of my adrenal glands, architect of balance. Your creation of essential hormones like cortisol and aldosterone gracefully navigates me through stress and sustains my body's fluid and salt balance. In your care, I find stability and the power to thrive.

Adrenal Medulla

With joy, I thank my adrenal medulla, the heart of my adrenal glands, for the rush of adrenaline and norepinephrine that sharpens my instincts and fuels my passions. Your vital surge in times of need empowers me to act swiftly, blending courage with clarity.

Pancreas (Endocrine part)

I am grateful for the endocrine portion of my pancreas, a hidden jewel in my abdomen. Your release of insulin and glucagon masterfully balances my blood sugar, gifting me with energy and harmony. In your subtle elegance, I savor life's sweetness, nourished and content.

Ovaries

I honor my ovaries, the cradle of creation and femininity within my pelvis. Your rhythms of estrogen and progesterone weave the tapestry of my cycles, embodying the essence of life's renewal. In your dance, I discover the profound mysteries of creation and the nurturing strength of womanhood.

Estrogen

My heart swells with gratitude for estrogen, the quintessence of femininity coursing through me. You sculpt my body's contours, protect my bones, and kindle the flame of my desire, painting my journey through life with the rich hues of emotion and connection. In your flow, I find the poetry of existence.

Progesterone

I cherish my progesterone, the serene nurturer, for enveloping me in calm and preparing my body for the miracle of life. You are the silent force that balances my well-being, soothing my spirit and enriching my journey to motherhood. In your gentle embrace, I find peace and the deep, nurturing connection to the cycle of life.

Testosterone

With gratitude, I acknowledge the subtle presence of testosterone within me, a spark of strength and vigor. Even in its quiet flow, it shapes my body's resilience, my mental clarity, and the delicate balance of my wellbeing. In this harmony, I celebrate the diversity of my femininity and the dynamic energy it bestows.

Follicle-Stimulating Hormone (FSH)

I am thankful for my follicle-stimulating hormone, the whisper that awakens life's potential within me. You guide the dawn of each cycle, fostering the seeds of future generations. In your cyclical call, I am connected to the rhythm of creation, participating in the dance of life with grace and anticipation.

Luteinizing Hormone (LH)

I express my gratitude to my luteinizing hormone, the herald of transformation within my body. Your precise timing ignites ovulation, a moment of pure potential. In this cycle of renewal, I see the strength of my body's natural wisdom, guiding me through the seasons of life with purpose and vitality.

Prolactin

To my prolactin, I offer my heartfelt thanks for the gift of nourishment and the bond it creates. You prepare me for the sacred act of motherhood, turning my body into a sanctuary of life. In your nurturing flow, I discover the depth of my capacity to love and sustain, a testament to the power of creation.

Growth Hormone

I am deeply grateful for my growth hormone, the architect of my body's form and strength. You sculpt the very foundation of my being, supporting renewal and vitality at every stage of life. In your enduring presence, I find the vigor to pursue my dreams and the resilience to face life's challenges with grace.

Adrenocorticotropic Hormone (ACTH)

With appreciation, I recognize my adrenocorticotropic hormone, the sentinel that ensures my resilience. You silently marshal the forces that protect and sustain me, guiding my body's response to stress with wisdom and care. In your vigilance, I find the courage to face each day with confidence and grace.

Thyroid-Stimulating Hormone (TSH)

I am thankful for my thyroid-stimulating hormone, the gentle encourager of my metabolic harmony. You orchestrate the symphony of my energy, ensuring that every cell in my body thrives. In your subtle guidance, I revel in the dynamism of life, energized and ready to embrace each new adventure.

Calcitonin

I express my gratitude for calcitonin, the guardian of my bones' fortitude. Your vigilant regulation of calcium fortifies my body, granting me strength and stability. In this steadfast protection, I move through life with assurance, grounded in the strength that supports me.

Parathyroid Hormone (PTH)

To my parathyroid hormone, I extend my deep appreciation for balancing the essence of my structure. You navigate the intricacies of calcium and phosphorus, ensuring my bones' vitality and my blood's vitality. In your careful balance, I find the foundation of my physical resilience, enabling me to stand tall and confident in my journey.

Insulin

I am profoundly grateful for insulin, the harmonious conductor of my body's energy orchestra. With grace, you guide glucose into my cells, fueling each moment of my life with the energy to thrive, to create, and to love. In your delicate balance, I find my vitality, a sweet symphony of life's endless possibilities.

Glucagon

To glucagon, my vigilant guardian in times of need, I offer my thanks. You are the key that unlocks my stored treasures, ensuring that my body is nourished and my spirit unbounded. In your careful watch, I am reassured, empowered to explore, dream, and discover with confidence and strength.

Melatonin

I cherish melatonin, the gentle lullaby of my being, for ushering in the night's embrace. In your soothing guidance, I find rest, renewal, and a sanctuary of dreams. Your rhythm, woven into the fabric of night, whispers the ancient song of restorative sleep, a gift of peace and rejuvenation.

Cortisol

With gratitude, I acknowledge cortisol, my body's sentinel in the dawn of challenges. Your alert presence guides me through the storms, a beacon of resilience and adaptability. In your strength, I am reminded of my capacity to rise, to face each day with courage and a heart ready to heal and grow.

Aldosterone

I am thankful for aldosterone, the subtle architect of my body's delicate balance. Through your wisdom, the oceans within me ebb and flow in perfect harmony, sustaining life's essence in every cell. In your gentle regulation, I find stability, a foundation of health that allows me to dance freely with life.

Epinephrine (Adrenaline)

To epinephrine, my spirited ally in moments of exhilaration and challenge, I give my heartfelt thanks. You surge within me as a wave of strength, sharpening my senses, quickening my pulse, and igniting the fire of my will. In your dynamic embrace, I discover the depths of my courage and the height of my joy.

Norepinephrine (Noradrenaline)

I am deeply grateful for norepinephrine, the vigilant keeper of my focus and drive. In your presence, my heart finds its rhythm, my mind its clarity, and my body its readiness to embrace the journey ahead. You weave the fabric of my resolve, empowering me to stand firm, to dream big, and to act with purpose.

Leptin

With appreciation, I honor leptin, the sage of satiety and balance within me. You speak the language of fullness, guiding my nourishment with wisdom and care. In your whispered counsel, I find harmony and satisfaction, a dance with nourishment that nurtures body, mind, and spirit.

Ghrelin

To ghrelin, the herald of hunger and desire, I extend my gratitude. You remind me of life's simplest pleasures, the joy of tasting, the warmth of being fed, the communion of meals shared. In your call, I am awakened to the beauty of appetite, the delight of nourishment, and the bond it weaves with the world around me.

Chapter 9: The Windows to the Soul

Admiring the Sensory Organs

Welcome to "Whisper of the Senses," a chapter that invites you to experience the world in its full sensory richness, celebrating the divine gifts of sight, sound, taste, touch, and smell. This journey is an homage to the miraculous ways we interact with our surroundings, a symphony of experiences that connect us to life's tapestry and to the Creator's boundless creativity.

In this chapter, we delve into the grace of our sensory organs, the portals through which beauty, harmony, and connection flow into our essence. Each sense, a channel of divine communication, enriches our understanding and appreciation of the world's wonders, from the intricate patterns of a leaf to the soothing sound of a gentle stream.

Let us embrace gratitude for our eyes, the beholders of light and color, for our ears, the receivers of melody and voice, for our skin, the canvas of touch and warmth, for our tongues, the tasters of bounty and nourishment, and for our noses, the discerners of fragrance and memory. These senses are not merely biological functions; they are gifts that inspire awe, evoke emotions, and foster connections, reminding us of God's omnipresence in the beauty that surrounds us.

"Whisper of the Senses" is an invitation to pause and reflect on the everyday miracles that fill our lives, to cultivate a deeper awareness of how we perceive and interact with the world. It's an encouragement to listen more attentively, look more closely, touch more tenderly, taste more mindfully, and inhale more deeply, appreciating the divine intricacy in every sensation.

Through gratitude for our sensory organs, we open our hearts to the endless splendor of creation, finding joy in the simple pleasures and a profound connection to the divine. This chapter aims not only to inform but to transform, guiding you to live more fully, more sensually, and with a greater sense of wonder and thankfulness.

Let the "Whisper of the Senses" reawaken your appreciation for the sensory gifts bestowed upon us, fostering a daily practice of gratitude that enriches your soul, enhances your well-being, and brings you closer to the sublime beauty of God's creation.

Eyes

My eyes, the mirrors to my soul, capture the beauty and essence of the world around me. Positioned like jewels on my face, they allow me to perceive the vibrancy of life, offering a window to the wonders that surround me. In their gaze, I find the power to communicate silently, sharing love, joy, and understanding without words.

Ears

I am grateful for my ears, the delicate sentinels on either side of my head, which channel the symphony of sounds that life offers. They grant me the joy of music, the voices of those I love, and the whispers of nature, enriching my existence with an invisible, yet palpable, tapestry of auditory delights.

Nose

My nose, a central feature on my face, serves as the gatekeeper to an array of scents that color my experiences. It guides me through life's moments with the subtle cues of fragrance, from the earthy smell of rain to the comforting aroma of home, making every breath a chapter in my story.

Tongue

For my tongue, I hold boundless appreciation. This versatile muscle not only articulates my thoughts and feelings but also navigates the rich landscape of flavors that nourish my body and soul. In its taste, I savor the sweetness of love and the zest of adventure, making each meal a celebration of life.

Skin

Gratitude envelops me for my skin, the soft armor that encases me, bridging the intimate divide between my inner world and the universe outside. It responds to the caress of a loved one and the warmth of the sun, making me feel connected, protected, and infinitely loved.

Retina

I am thankful for my retina, the intricate canvas at the back of my eyes where light transforms into the magic of sight. It captures the beauty of a sunset and the twinkle of starlight, allowing me to paint my memories with the colors and shapes of the world.

Cochlea

Deep appreciation for my cochlea, the spiral chamber in my ears that translates sound waves into the melodies of life. It allows me to hear the laughter of friends, the soothing cadence of a comforting voice, and the harmony of music, enriching my world with the dimension of sound.

Olfactory Bulbs

My olfactory bulbs, perched atop my nasal cavity, I cherish for unlocking the memories and emotions carried by scents. They navigate me through the seasons of life with the fragrance of blooming flowers, the crispness of autumn air, and the comforting scent of a familiar place.

Taste Buds

I am filled with joy for my taste buds, the tiny sentinels of flavor that dance upon my tongue. They celebrate the diversity of the world's bounty, from the sweetness of fruit to the complexity of spices, making each meal a journey of discovery and delight.

Touch Receptors

With warmth, I honor my touch receptors, scattered like stars beneath the surface of my skin. They allow me to feel the embrace of a loved one, the texture of fabric, and the brush of the wind, connecting me to the tangible and the tender in life.

Cornea

Gratitude shines for my cornea, the clear dome that covers the eye, focusing light and allowing me to see the world in crisp clarity. It is the lens through which I witness life's beauty, making me feel grateful for every sunrise, every smile, and every moment of connection.

Lens

I cherish my lens, the transparent jewel within my eye, adjusting and focusing light to capture life's moments with precision. It grants me the clarity to see my path, to read the words of wisdom, and to behold the faces of those I hold dear.

Optic Nerve

I am profoundly thankful for my optic nerve, the vital link that carries the gift of vision from my eyes to my brain. It weaves the fabric of my visual experiences, allowing me to see, learn, and remember, making me feel connected to the world in all its splendor.

Auditory Nerves

With heartfelt appreciation, I acknowledge my auditory nerves, the carriers of sound from my ears to my mind. They resonate with the vibrations of life, from harmonious melodies to meaningful conversations, enriching my existence with the richness of sound.

Semicircular Canals

I extend my gratitude to my semicircular canals, the architects of balance nestled within my inner ear. They choreograph the dance of stability, allowing me to move gracefully through life's twists and turns, making every step a testament to harmony and grace.

Olfactory Epithelium

For my olfactory epithelium, a delicate tapestry within my nose, I am profoundly thankful. It captures the essence of fragrances, from the rain-soaked earth to the warmth of baked bread, enriching my life with an invisible palette of scents.

Papillae

My papillae, the tiny guardians of taste on my tongue, earn my heartfelt appreciation. They unlock the flavors of the world, from the sharpness of citrus to the richness of chocolate, making each meal an adventure in joy and discovery.

Hair Follicles

Gratitude blossoms for my hair follicles, the cradle of every strand of hair on my body. They not only provide the canvas for expression through my hair but also offer the delicate touch of sensation, connecting me to the world in the most intimate ways.

Sweat Glands

I cherish my sweat glands, for they are the unsung heroes regulating my body's harmony with the environment. Through their silent work, I engage with the world energetically, feeling refreshed and invigorated, ready to embrace life's challenges with poise.

Sebaceous Glands

To my sebaceous glands, I offer gratitude for their role in keeping my skin nourished and protected. They produce the oils that give my skin its softness and luster, making me feel beautiful and confident in my own skin.

Rods and Cones

My rods and cones, the stewards of light and color in my eyes, receive my adoration. They capture the spectrum of life's beauty, allowing me to revel in the nuances of day and night, shadow and light, making every view a masterpiece of perception.

Eustachian Tube

I am thankful for my Eustachian tube, the silent regulator of balance and pressure in my ears. It keeps the symphony of sounds clear and the harmony of equilibrium intact, allowing me to listen and move with ease and comfort.

Tympanic Membrane

For my tympanic membrane, my eardrum, I hold deep appreciation. It vibrates with the rhythms of life, translating sound waves into the music of existence, letting me tune into the melody of the world around me.

Vestibular System

Gratitude flows for my vestibular system, the compass within my inner ear that guides my sense of movement and balance. It allows me to navigate the world with confidence, ensuring that I stand strong and move smoothly, no matter the path I take.

Fovea

I treasure my fovea, the central pit of my retina, for its role in granting me sharp, central vision. It allows me to focus on the details that matter, from the words on a page to the expressions on the faces of those I love, making every look a gift of clarity.

Lacrimal Glands

My lacrimal glands, reservoirs of tears, are cherished for their role in expressing the depth of my emotions. They cleanse my eyes and soul, allowing for the release of joy, sorrow, and the beauty of vulnerability, making each tear a drop of my humanity.

Macula

With joy, I honor my macula, the area of precise vision in my retina. It enables me to see the fine details of the world, from the delicate hues of a flower to the intricate patterns of art, enriching my appreciation of beauty and detail.

Ciliary Body

I express gratitude for my ciliary body, the ring of tissue in my eye that focuses vision. It adjusts the lens of my eye, allowing me to see near and far, making the act of seeing a continuous miracle of adaptation and clarity.

Olfactory Tract

To my olfactory tract, I give thanks for transporting the scents of the world to my brain. It navigates me through the rich landscape of aromas, connecting memories and emotions, making every scent a storyline in the narrative of my life.

Gustatory Cortex

My gustatory cortex, the realm of taste perception in my brain, earns my gratitude. It interprets the flavors of existence, from the sweetness of success to the bitterness of challenge, teaching me to savor life's banquet with resilience and joy.

Chapter 10: The Canvas of Identity

Embracing the Integumentary System

D ive into "Embrace of Elegance," where we celebrate the protective grace and exquisite beauty of the Integumentary System. This chapter is a poetic ode to the skin, hair, and nails—the guardians and storytellers of our bodies, a canvas upon which our life stories unfold. Each element of this system not only shields us but also presents us in our unique essence, reflecting the Creator's artistry in every texture, hue, and contour.

As you embark on this journey, feel the gentle touch of air on your skin, the resilience of your nails, and the flow of your hair. These experiences are invitations to marvel at the sophisticated design and purpose behind our body's largest organ system, a testament to divine ingenuity and care.

The Integumentary System is our interface with the world, a delicate yet durable barrier that engages in a constant dance of protection and expression. It regulates, senses, and communicates, playing a pivotal role in our interaction with the environment and in our expression of individuality.

This chapter encourages you to nourish a deep gratitude for your skin's ability to heal and rejuvenate, for your hair's capacity to express and transform, and for your nails' strength and growth. Through appreciating these aspects, we acknowledge our body's silent work in protecting and defining us, facilitating a connection to the world and to the divine.

"Embrace of Elegance" invites you to explore the profound spiritual symbolism embedded within the Integumentary System—a shield of faith, a mantle of uniqueness, and a testament to resilience. It's an encouragement to care for and appreciate this system not just for its functional brilliance but for its aesthetic beauty and its role in shaping our interaction with the divine and the earthly.

Let this chapter be a transformative path to seeing your skin, hair, and nails as visible signs of God's grace and wisdom, fostering a daily ritual of gratitude that enhances your self-esteem and spiritual connection. Through the lens of thankfulness, we can perceive our integumentary system as a divine gift, a source of joy and a bridge to a deeper understanding of our place in the universe.

Skin

I revel in the joy of my skin, my body's loving embrace. It shields me, tells my story, and connects me with the world in a tender dance of sensations. In its resilience, I see my own strength, feeling endlessly beautiful and powerfully cherished.

Hair

Gratitude fills me for my hair, the expression of my soul's language. It offers me the canvas to showcase my inner beauty and strength to the world. Through its versatility, I feel empowered, beautiful, and deeply connected to my personal identity.

Nails

My nails, the protectors of my fingertips, bring me joy with their grace and strength. They are a reflection of my health and a medium for artistic expression, making me feel cared for, elegant, and creatively vibrant.

Sweat Glands

I am thankful for my sweat glands, a testament to my body's wisdom in harmony and balance. They empower me to embrace life's passions with vigor, cooling and cleansing me. In their function, I find a profound connection to well-being, feeling refreshed and energetically alive.

Sebaceous Glands

My sebaceous glands, the nurturers of my skin, wrap me in a soft glow of health. Their gentle oiling keeps me radiant and protected, a symbol of the body's loving care. Feeling moisturized and supple, I am reminded of my intrinsic beauty and the joy of being nurtured.

Hair Follicles

Deep appreciation for my hair follicles, from which springs the essence of my identity. They grow and renew the threads of my story, allowing me to wear my strength and femininity with pride. In their cycle, I am inspired by the beauty of change, feeling renewed and vibrantly alive.

Epidermis

For my epidermis, my gratitude knows no bounds. It stands as my first line of defense, a delicate barrier that connects me to the world while protecting my inner self. In its resilience, I find a reflection of my own strength, feeling beautifully secure and visibly radiant.

Dermis

I honor my dermis, the supportive layer beneath, rich with life's textures. It houses the fibers of my being, lending elasticity and sensitivity, allowing me to feel the world deeply. In its vitality, I discover the foundations of youth and beauty, feeling supple and deeply connected.

Hypodermis (Subcutaneous Fat)

My hypodermis, a layer of warmth and energy, earns my heartfelt gratitude. It shapes the soft contours of my femininity, providing comfort and protection. In its gentle embrace, I see the beauty of form and function, feeling embraced by love and the warmth of self-acceptance.

Melanocytes

Grateful for my melanocytes, the painters of my skin's color, guardians against the sun's embrace. They celebrate diversity and resilience, coloring me in shades of health and heritage. In their care, I find joy in my unique hue, feeling beautifully protected and wonderfully unique.

Keratinocytes

I am thankful for my keratinocytes, architects of my outermost protection. They renew and defend, a testament to the body's self-healing grace. In their resilience, I am reminded of my ability to recover and flourish, feeling empowered, secure, and radiantly healthy.

Langerhans Cells

Appreciation envelops my Langerhans cells, the vigilant defenders within my skin. Their silent guardianship against external foes makes me feel safe and attentively cared for. In their protection, I find a deep sense of security, feeling loved by my body's own wisdom.

Merkel Cells

To my Merkel cells, I offer my gratitude for the gift of delicate touch. They unlock the world's textures, from the softness of silk to the warmth of a loving hand. In their sensitivity, I am connected to life's exquisite details, feeling deeply loved and profoundly alive.

Meissner's Corpuscles

I cherish my Meissner's corpuscles, nestled within the tips of my fingers, enabling the joy of texture and the gentle whisper of touch. In their sensitivity, I am gifted with the ability to feel the world in its splendid detail, making me feel profoundly connected and vibrantly alive.

Pacinian Corpuscles

Gratitude for my Pacinian corpuscles, deep sensors of pressure and vibration, for they connect me to the rhythm of life. Their presence allows me to experience the grounding touch of the earth and the comforting embrace of loved ones, filling me with a sense of security and love.

Free Nerve Endings

I am thankful for my free nerve endings, the delicate threads that weave through my skin, alerting me to warmth, cold, and touch. They are the heralds of sensation, making me feel alive to the world's caress, deeply in tune with my surroundings and the tapestry of life.

Arrector Pili Muscles

My arrector pili muscles, the artists of goosebumps, earn my appreciation for their role in the dance of emotions. They react to cold, touch, and feelings, a physical manifestation of awe or excitement, reminding me of the beauty in the body's intuitive expressions.

Blood Vessels in the Skin

Deep thanks to the blood vessels in my skin, the rivers of life that nourish and color my appearance. They bring warmth and vitality, a blush of health and emotion, making me feel beautifully alive, radiant with the glow of well-being.

Lymph Vessels

I honor my lymph vessels, the silent pathways of cleansing and immunity within my skin. Their diligent work in protecting and purifying me fills me with gratitude, making me feel cherished and safeguarded by my body's natural grace.

Collagen Fibers

Gratitude fills me for my collagen fibers, the scaffolding of my skin's strength and elasticity. They hold me together, a testament to resilience and youth, allowing me to face the world with confidence, feeling firm and beautifully vibrant.

Elastin Fibers

I am grateful for my elastin fibers, the springs that give my skin its ability to stretch and bounce back. In their resilience, I find the joy of movement and expression, feeling supple, free, and wonderfully elastic in the dance of life.

Pores

My pores, the tiny gateways of breath for my skin, deserve my thanks. They release sweat, cool me down, and help me glow, a symbol of the skin's natural beauty and function, making me feel authentically radiant and healthily vibrant.

Acne

Even in the presence of acne, I find a moment to appreciate my skin's signal to seek balance and care. It teaches me the importance of nurturing myself both inside and out. With every act of gratitude, I envision these signs gently fading away, leaving my skin clear, radiant, and beautifully healthy.

Stretch Marks

I see my stretch marks as ribbons of life's experiences, each one a mark of growth, change, or renewal. They remind me of my journey's depth and the beauty in every phase of life. With every expression of gratitude, I feel these symbols of my story blend more harmoniously into my skin, celebrating the resilience and elasticity of my being.

Cellulite

Gratitude for my cellulite, a natural aspect of my body's landscape. It reminds me of the beauty in imperfection and the importance of self-love and acceptance, making me feel grounded in my femininity and uniquely beautiful.

UV Protection Mechanisms (Melanin)

I am profoundly thankful for melanin, my skin's natural protector against the sun's rays. It guards me with a loving embrace, allowing me to enjoy the light while staying shielded, making me feel cared for and beautifully resilient.

Cutaneous Sensation

Deep appreciation for the gift of cutaneous sensation, the magic of feeling the world through my skin. It connects me to the breeze, the warmth of the sun, and the tenderness of touch, making me feel deeply alive and in a constant embrace with the universe.

Thermoregulation

I honor my body's ability to thermoregulate, a marvel of balance and adaptation. It keeps me comfortable through the seasons, a silent yet profound testament to the body's wisdom, making me feel harmoniously in sync with the rhythms of nature.

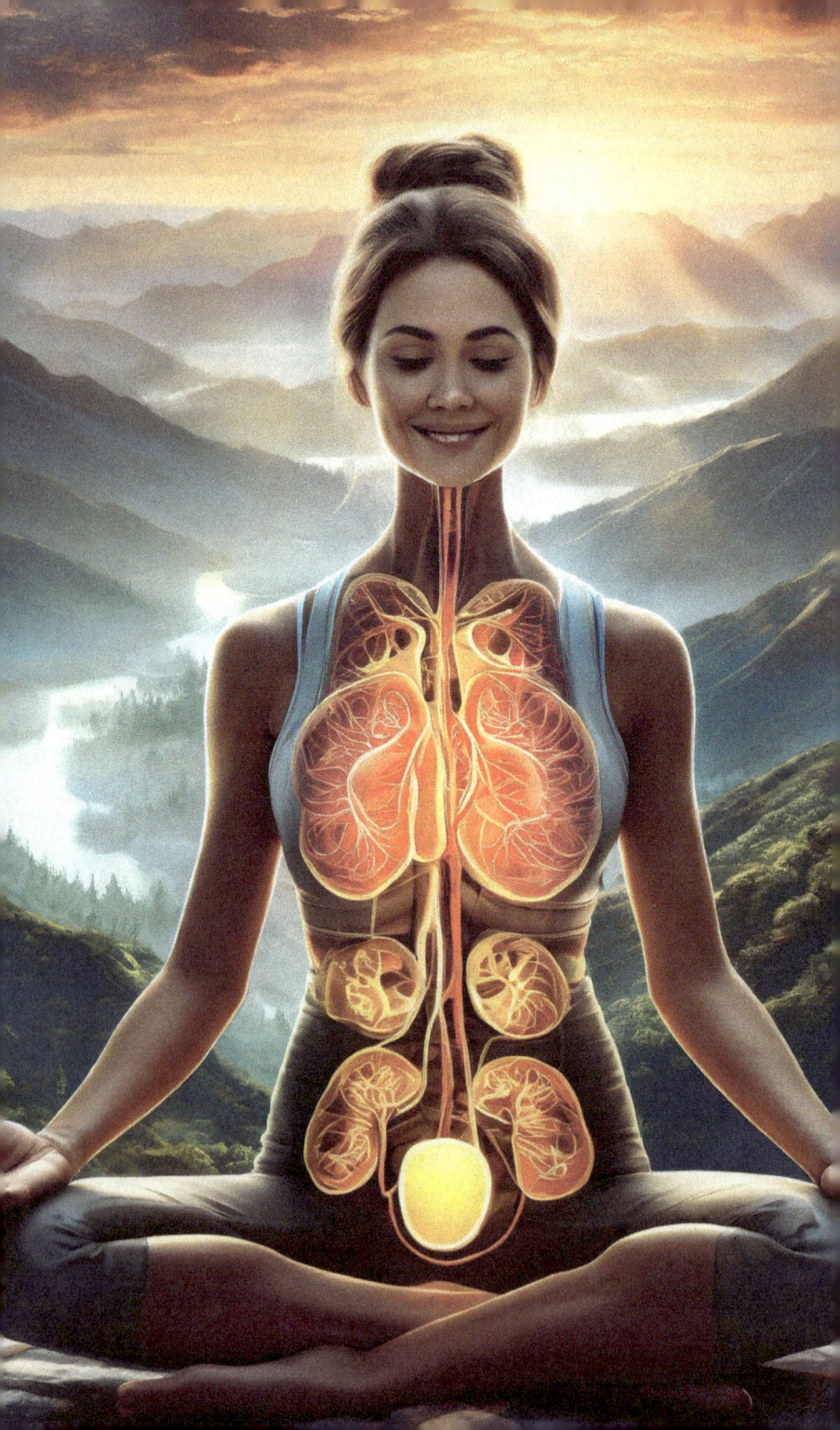

Chapter 11: The Pathways of Purification

Acknowledging the Excretory System

S tep into "Purifying Grace," a chapter that guides you through the Excretory System with reverence and gratitude for its vital role in cleansing and renewal. This journey illuminates the divine wisdom embedded in our body's natural purification processes, a testament to God's design for health, balance, and well-being. The Excretory System, in its quiet efficiency, mirrors the cycle of life—taking in, transforming, and releasing—emphasizing the beauty of letting go that which no longer serves us.

As we delve into the wonders of this system, from the kidneys' meticulous filtration to the lungs' breath of release, let us be moved by the elegance of our body's capacity to purify itself. This intricate dance of absorption and excretion is a divine orchestration, ensuring that we remain balanced, vibrant, and ready to receive new blessings.

In embracing gratitude for the Excretory System, we not only celebrate the physical benefits of detoxification and balance but also draw parallels to our spiritual journey. Just as our bodies are designed to release waste and toxins, our spirits are called to shed burdens, worries, and negativity, allowing for rejuvenation and growth.

"Purifying Grace" encourages you to reflect on the processes of release and renewal within your own life, recognizing them as gifts of divine love and care. It invites a practice of mindfulness about what we hold onto and what we let go, fostering a healthier, more harmonious existence.

Through the lens of gratitude, let this chapter inspire you to honor your body's natural wisdom, to cultivate habits that support purification and balance, and to embrace the spiritual lessons of cleansing and renewal. The Excretory System, in its humble yet crucial function, becomes a powerful metaphor for spiritual well-being, teaching us about the beauty of transformation and the grace of release.

Let "Purifying Grace" be a reminder of the divine presence in the most basic functions of our bodies, guiding us toward a deeper appreciation of our physical and spiritual cleansing. Through this appreciation, we discover a path to a more empowered and enlightened self, grounded in the loving embrace of God's design.

Kidneys

I am filled with gratitude for my kidneys, nestled within my lower back, guardians of balance and purity. They meticulously filter my blood, ensuring harmony within. In their function, I find a profound sense of well-being, feeling cleansed, revitalized, and deeply cared for.

Ureters

Thankful for my ureters, the diligent pathways that carry the essence of purification from my kidneys to my bladder. Their seamless transport allows me to release what no longer serves me, making me feel light, refreshed, and beautifully renewed.

Urinary Bladder

I cherish my urinary bladder, a reservoir of release and relief nestled within my pelvis. It gracefully holds and then liberates, allowing me to feel unburdened and free. In this cycle of renewal, I find strength, comfort, and a deep sense of inner peace.

Urethra

Gratitude illuminates my urethra, the final channel through which purification flows, marking the completion of an essential journey. It empowers me to release and renew, making me feel empowered, clean, and vibrantly alive.

Nephrons

My nephrons, the microscopic miracles within my kidneys, earn my heartfelt appreciation. They filter my blood with precision, a testament to the body's intricate design, making me feel marvelously complex and wonderfully efficient.

Renal Arteries

I am thankful for my renal arteries, the vital conduits supplying blood to my kidneys. Their pulsing vitality brings the promise of renewal, making me feel supported and nourished by life's unending flow.

Renal Veins

Deep appreciation for my renal veins, the return vessels of clarity and balance from my kidneys to my heart. In their return, I see the cycle of life's energies, making me feel connected, cleansed, and lovingly restored.

Glomerulus

For my glomerulus, the filtering heart of each nephron, I hold profound gratitude. You initiate the process of purification, a delicate balance of letting go and holding on, making me feel intricately woven into the fabric of life.

Bowman's Capsule

Gratitude to my Bowman's capsule, the cradle of filtration, where waste and water first part from the vital. In this delicate separation, I find the essence of discernment, feeling purified and gracefully balanced.

Proximal Convoluted Tubule

I appreciate my proximal convoluted tubule, where the journey of reabsorption and cleansing begins. It reminds me of the body's wisdom in conservation, making me feel resourceful, nurtured, and wonder-fully efficient.

Loop of Henle

Thankful for my Loop of Henle, the pathway of concentration and purification within my nephrons. Its delicate balance of salts and water mirrors life's own balances, making me feel harmoniously attuned and deeply cleansed.

Distal Convoluted Tubule

I honor my distal convoluted tubule, a key stage in the refinement and rebalancing of my body's fluids. In its selective return, I find a metaphor for life's choices, making me feel discerning, empowered, and healthily vibrant.

Collecting Ducts

My collecting ducts, the final gatherers of what will be released, receive my gratitude. They symbolize the unity of purpose and the joy of release, making me feel cohesive, light, and refreshingly renewed.

Renal Cortex

Gratitude for my renal cortex, the outer layer of my kidneys, rich with the potential for filtration. In its structure, I see the strength and resilience of my body, feeling protected, supported, and beautifully vital.

Renal Medulla

I am grateful for my renal medulla, the inner sanctum of my kidneys, where concentration reaches its peak. Its deep work reminds me of the depths of my own being, feeling purified, focused, and intensely alive.

Renal Pelvis

Deep appreciation for my renal pelvis, the collecting chamber within my kidney. It represents the gathering of experiences, the precursor to release, making me feel prepared, cleansed, and ready for what comes next.

Sweat Glands

For my sweat glands, the silent purifiers through the skin, I am profoundly thankful. They cool and cleanse my body, a reminder of the beauty in detoxification, making me feel radiant, healthy, and beautifully alive.

Liver (in its role in detoxification)

My liver, the master alchemist, transforms what I consume into nutrients and neutralizes toxins with silent diligence. Its constant care fills me with awe, making me feel cherished, nurtured, and vibrantly healthy.

Large Intestine

I cherish my large intestine, the final curator of what I absorb and what I let go. It teaches me the importance of release and the value of holding onto only what nourishes me, making me feel light, balanced, and profoundly renewed.

Chapter 12: The Wellspring of Creation

Cherishing the Female Reproductive System

Welcome to "The Sacred Womb," a chapter devoted to the reverence and admiration of the female reproductive system, an exquisite embodiment of creation, renewal, and the divine power of life itself. This portion of our journey invites us to marvel at the intricate beauty and profound capability of the female body to nurture and bring forth life, reflecting God's magnificent design and the sacredness of motherhood.

As you immerse yourself in this chapter, allow yourself to feel a deep connection to the divine artistry and wisdom that crafted such a complex and miraculous system. From the gentle whispers of ovulation to the strength of the uterus, each aspect of the female reproductive system is a testament to the miracle of life and the embodiment of God's love and creative power.

This exploration is not merely an acknowledgment of the biological functions but a celebration of the feminine essence and its vital role in the cycle of life. It is an invitation to honor and express gratitude for the sacred processes that dwell within, recognizing them as sources of strength, femininity, and divine connection.

Engaging with "The Sacred Womb" encourages us to view the female reproductive system with awe and respect, acknowledging its capabilities not just in the realm of procreation but as a central part of our identity and womanhood. It serves as a reminder of our connection to the cycle of life, the power of creation that flows through us, and the divine grace that guides these processes.

In expressing gratitude for our reproductive system, we open our hearts to the healing and nurturing energies it represents. We acknowledge the system's role in our journey of womanhood, from the rhythmic cycles that remind us of life's constant ebb and flow to the profound capability of giving birth to new life and ideas.

Let "The Sacred Womb" deepen your appreciation for the female body's divine intricacy and the miraculous cycles that unfold within it. May this chapter inspire you to embrace the beauty of your reproductive system, to recognize its role in your spiritual and emotional journey, and to cherish it as a symbol of life, renewal, and divine femininity.

Through gratitude and reverence, we not only celebrate the physical attributes of the female reproductive system but also embrace the spiritual lessons and empowerment it offers. Let this chapter be a pathway to a more profound connection with the divine, a celebration of femininity, and a commitment to nurturing the sacred within.

Ovaries

I am deeply grateful for my ovaries, the wellsprings of life nestled within me. They are the cradle of creation, harboring the potential for new life and orchestrating the rhythm of my femininity through the dance of hormones, making me feel profoundly connected to the cycle of life.

Fallopian Tubes

Thankful for my fallopian tubes, the graceful pathways of connection and possibility. They guide the union of life's beginnings, a testament to hope and continuity. In their delicate embrace, I find the magic of potential, feeling deeply attuned to the miracle of creation.

Uterus

I cherish my uterus, a haven of strength and transformation. It is the sacred chamber of nurturing and growth, holding the promise of future generations. In its resilience and capacity for renewal, I feel a powerful connection to the essence of womanhood and the cycle of life.

Endometrium

My endometrium, the lining that prepares for life's potential each month, earns my heartfelt gratitude. It is the canvas of receptivity and renewal, ready to nurture new beginnings. In its cyclic renewal, I see the beauty of resilience and regeneration, feeling deeply nurtured.

Myometrium

Gratitude envelops my myometrium, the muscular layer of my uterus, for its strength and flexibility. It supports and protects, a symbol of my body's incredible ability to adapt and embrace life's changes. In its power, I find a reflection of my own strength and adaptability.

Cervix

I am thankful for my cervix, the guardian at the gateway of life, balancing protection with the passage of creation. It stands as a testament to my body's wisdom, making me feel secure and marvelously intricate in the design of my femininity.

Vagina

Deep appreciation for my vagina, the channel of birth and pleasure, for its role in intimacy and connection. It stands as a testament to the power of birth, the gateway through which life emerges. In its essence, I find the joy of being, feeling embraced by life's most intimate moments.

Fimbriae

I appreciate my fimbriae, the delicate fingers that guide life's beginnings on their journey. They work with silent precision, a testament to the intricacies of creation. In their gentle guidance, I see the dance of possibility, feeling awe at the precision of life's initiation.

Ovum (Egg Cells)

Deep thanks to my ovum, the sacred vessels of potential. Each one holds the promise of life, a miracle in miniature. In their existence, I am connected to the continuum of generations, feeling the profound weight and wonder of creation.

Follicles

Gratitude for my follicles, the nurturing environments that cradle the seeds of life. They are the stages of preparation, anticipation, and hope, making me feel intimately involved in the cycle of life, marveling at the beauty of potential.

Corpus Luteum

I am grateful for my corpus luteum, the temporary yet vital creator of harmony and support for new life. In its role, I find a symbol of my body's commitment to nurturing and balance, feeling supported and harmonized within the cycle of creation.

Estrogen and Progesterone

For estrogen and progesterone, the harmonizers of my being, I express boundless gratitude. They weave the tapestry of my health, mood, and well-being, coloring my days with the hues of vitality. In their flow, I find the essence of my femininity, feeling balanced, vibrant, and deeply connected to the rhythms of life.

Hymen

Gratitude for my hymen, a part of my unique anatomy, marking passages and phases of life. It stands as a testament to the diversity of female experiences, making me feel connected to the shared journey of womanhood.

G-Spot

I cherish my G-Spot, a symbol of pleasure and self-discovery within me. It invites exploration and connection, deepening the understanding of my own desires. In its presence, I celebrate the joy of intimacy, feeling empowered and deeply attuned to the wonders of my body.

Vulva

For my vulva, including the labia majora and minora, I hold immense gratitude. It is the symbol of my femininity, the outer expression of my identity as a woman. In its unique beauty, I celebrate my individuality and the joy of sensuality, feeling beautiful and empowered.

Clitoris

I cherish my clitoris, a source of joy and discovery, the beacon of pleasure. It reminds me of the capacity for delight and self-knowledge, making me feel vibrant, empowered, and deeply connected to my body's potential for happiness.

Bartholin's Glands

Gratitude for my Bartholin's glands, the silent providers of comfort and ease, ensuring the balance of nature's lubrication. In their subtle work, I am reminded of the body's care in every aspect of health and pleasure, feeling wonderfully cared for and seamlessly whole.

Mammary Glands (Breasts)

I honor my mammary glands, the essence of nourishment and symbol of maternal love. They represent the strength of nurturing and the bond of life, making me feel powerfully connected to the cycle of care and the deep wellspring of affection.

Menstrual Cycle

With reverence, I acknowledge my menstrual cycle, a rhythm of renewal and cleansing. It is the pulse of my connection to the universe's cycles, a reminder of my body's incredible ability to regenerate and prepare. In its phases, I find the power of adaptation and renewal, feeling in harmony with the natural world.

Chapter 13: The Guardians of Health

Praising the Lymphatic System

S tep into the realm of "The Flow of Harmony," a chapter dedicated to the lymphatic system, an often-underappreciated marvel of our body that plays a pivotal role in maintaining health, balance, and harmony within. This system, a silent guardian of our well-being, mirrors the gentle, yet powerful, grace of divine providence, cleansing and protecting us with a subtlety that belies its strength.

In the divine wisdom that shapes our existence, the lymphatic system stands as a testament to the intricate balance and interconnectedness of all life. It is a reflection of God's foresight and care, designed to purify and defend, ensuring that every cell in our body resonates with the vibrancy of health and the tranquility of a harmoniously functioning whole.

As you delve into this chapter, let each word guide you to a deeper understanding and appreciation of this intricate network. Visualize the lymph flowing through your body, a serene river of purity, washing away toxins and nurturing your cells with the essence of life itself. This visualization is not merely an exercise in gratitude but a profound connection to the unseen forces that sustain us, orchestrated by a divine hand.

The lymphatic system, with its lymph nodes, vessels, and fluids, serves not just in physical detoxification but as a spiritual metaphor for renewal and cleansing. It reminds us that just as our bodies are designed to purge what no longer serves us, so too should we release emotional and spiritual burdens that weigh us down, trusting in God's plan for our renewal and growth.

This chapter is an invitation to honor the quiet work of the lymphatic system, recognizing it as a vital component of our health and a symbol of the divine care that envelops us. By acknowledging and expressing gratitude for this gentle yet powerful system, we align ourselves with the natural rhythms of our body and the universe, opening our hearts to the healing and balance it offers.

Let "The Flow of Harmony" inspire you to embrace the lymphatic system as a key to physical and spiritual well-being. May this chapter empower you to foster a deeper connection with your body, to live in gratitude for the unseen blessings that sustain you, and to walk a path that reflects the beauty, balance, and harmony of God's creation.

In celebrating the lymphatic system, we celebrate the divine wisdom that interweaves our physical and spiritual selves, reminding us of the grace that flows through every aspect of our being, cleansing, nurturing, and harmonizing, in accordance with the divine path laid out for us.

Lymph

I am filled with gratitude for my lymph, the clear, nourishing fluid that flows through my body, embodying the essence of purity and renewal. It carries away toxins and brings to my cells the gift of health, making me feel cleansed, vibrant, and lovingly cared for.

Lymph Nodes

Deep appreciation for my lymph nodes, stationed like vigilant sentinels throughout my body. They are the fortresses of my immunity, filtering lymph and safeguarding my health. In their resilience, I find a reflection of my own strength, feeling protected and powerfully serene.

Lymphatic Vessels

Thankful for my lymphatic vessels, the intricate network that weaves through my body, a testament to life's delicate balance. They ensure the flow of health and harmony, connecting every part of me in a dance of wellbeing, making me feel gracefully interconnected and whole.

Thymus

I cherish my thymus, nestled in my chest, the cradle of my immune warriors. It educates and prepares them to defend my well-being, a foundation of my vitality. In its nurturing role, I feel empowered, ready to face the world with confidence and a profound sense of security.

Spleen

Gratitude to my spleen, the diligent purifier of my blood and keeper of immunity. Its quiet work supports my body in silence, a constant guardian of my health. In its vigilance, I am reassured, enveloped in a blanket of protection and wellness.

Tonsils

My tonsils, the guardians of my throat, receive my heartfelt thanks. They stand as the first line of defense against inhaled or ingested invaders, a symbol of my body's proactive care. In their protection, I find my voice strengthened, feeling loved and valiantly defended.

Adenoids

Appreciation for my adenoids, the silent watchers over my respiratory health. They filter the air I breathe, a subtle yet potent shield against harm. In their presence, I breathe easier, feeling the gentle embrace of health with every breath.

Peyer's Patches

I am grateful for my Peyer's patches, embedded in the lining of my intestines, vigilant in their watch over my digestive health. They are the unseen heroes of my immunity, making me feel deeply nourished and attentively cared for from within.

Appendix

For my appendix, a repository of beneficial bacteria, I hold a sense of wonder and gratitude. Its role in immune support, once a mystery, now reveals the intricate design of my body's defenses, making me feel marvelously complex and beautifully resilient.

Bone Marrow

Deep thanks to my bone marrow, the wellspring of life within my bones. It births the cells that form the backbone of my immunity, a profound source of strength and renewal. In its essence, I find the roots of my vitality, feeling grounded and abundantly alive.

Lymphocytes

I honor my lymphocytes, including T cells and B cells, the diligent warriors of my immune system. They navigate my body with precision, a dynamic force against challenges. In their commitment, I see the embodiment of love and protection, feeling beautifully safeguarded.

Natural Killer (NK) Cells

Gratitude for my Natural Killer (NK) cells, the swift responders in my immune system's arsenal. Their readiness to defend and protect me at a moment's notice fills me with confidence, feeling powerfully secure and cherished.

Lymphatic Capillaries

Thankful for my lymphatic capillaries, the finest threads in the tapestry of my lymphatic system. They draw away the unwanted, ensuring clarity and cleanliness, making me feel light, purified, and gracefully balanced.

Cisterna Chyli

I appreciate my cisterna chyli, a serene reservoir where lymph gathers strength on its journey. It symbolizes the depth of my internal care, pooling resources for my protection, making me feel nurtured and profoundly supported.

Thoracic Duct

For my thoracic duct, the majestic conduit returning purified lymph to my bloodstream, I am deeply thankful. Its role in sustaining my equilibrium makes me feel harmoniously connected, revitalized, and whole.

Right Lymphatic Duct

Gratitude for my right lymphatic duct, a key channel guiding lymph's return. It ensures that the guardianship of my health is balanced and complete, making me feel cared for, secure, and beautifully harmonized.

Mucosa-associated Lymphoid Tissue (MALT)

My MALT, the discreet protector of my body's gateways, earns my heartfelt appreciation. It watches over me with gentle vigilance, making me feel loved and safeguarded in every moment, a quiet sentinel of my well-being.

Gut-associated Lymphoid Tissue (GALT)

I am grateful for my GALT, the guardian of my digestive tract's immunity. Its presence reminds me of the intimate connection between health and nourishment, feeling deeply cared for and resilient in the face of life's ebb and flow.

Afterword

As we gently close the final chapter of "Grateful Lady," it's a moment to pause and reflect, not just on the words and pages that have passed beneath our eyes, but on the journey itself. If the journey through these pages has inspired even a whisper of gratitude in your heart, then indeed, this endeavor has found its purpose. Writing "Grateful Lady," alongside its counterpart, "Grateful Man," has been an odyssey of discovery, revealing the unique intricacies that distinguish and celebrate the feminine spirit and form.

This exploration, rooted in gratitude and wonder, aimed to illuminate the inherent beauty and power within the female body, showcasing it as a divine masterpiece. As a man venturing into the sanctity of the feminine experience, I found myself on a path of profound learning. It highlighted how intricately our lives are woven with threads of divine intention, teaching me the significance of each aspect that comprises the female form.

This journey was not one I walked alone; it was guided by the light of the Divine and supported by the loving presence of my wife, Rahila, whose encouragement was a constant source of strength. Moreover, it was enriched by you, the reader, whose engagement with these pages has woven your spirit into the tapestry of this book's life.

I extend my deepest gratitude to you, the reader, for your willingness to embark on this journey with me. Your engagement transforms this book from mere words on paper into a shared exploration of gratitude. It's my sincere hope that "Grateful Lady" finds a cherished place beside your bed, serving as both a nightly reflection on the beauty and strength that defines womanhood and a morning invocation of gratitude to start your day. In this way, our shared path of discovery and appreciation doesn't conclude here but continues to unfold with each day, perhaps indefinitely.

The act of gratitude, as explored in these pages, is more than an acknowledgment; it's a celebration of the marvels of our existence, a practice that can transform how we perceive the world around us and our place within it. "Grateful Lady" is intended to be a companion on this journey, a source of comfort, inspiration, and continual reflection.

Our voyage together through the realms of gratitude signifies a connection that extends beyond the final page. This book, and the journey it represents, is a commitment to seeing the divine in the everyday, to cherishing our bodies as temples of spirit and life, and to recognizing the beauty in ourselves and in the connections that grace our lives.

With this afterword, I invite you to carry forward the spirit of gratitude that "Grateful Lady" seeks to instill. May it serve as a beacon, guiding you towards a deeper appreciation for the wonders of your being and the world around you. Our journey of gratitude is an ongoing narrative, one that I am honored to share with you.

If the journey through 'Grateful Lady' has enriched your life with a newfound appreciation for the beauty and complexity of the female form, I warmly invite you to share this experience with others. By passing on the light of gratitude, you help illuminate the path for more souls to discover the joy and fulfillment that comes from celebrating our divine craftsmanship. With heartfelt appreciation for our shared path and anticipation for the endless discoveries still to come.

Stay Connected

The journey with "Grateful Lady" and "Grateful Man" doesn't end here. Your stories and experiences can illuminate the path for others and deepen our collective exploration of gratitude. I invite you to share how these books have touched your life and to continue this dialogue of appreciation.

Your personal reflections, stories of gratitude, and insights are what transform this journey from a solitary path into a shared adventure. I warmly invite you to share how these books have inspired you, and to continue this dialogue of appreciation and self-discovery.

Quick Ways to Stay in Touch:

 Scan to Visit My Amazon Author Page

 Scan to Visit My Website

 Scan to Visit My Facebook Page

www.ingramcontent.com/pod-product-compliance
Lightning Source LLC
Chambersburg PA
CBHW071148120626
46546CB00006B/2172

* 9 7 8 1 9 6 4 5 4 8 0 0 5 *